RETRIEVER TRAINING:
A BACK-TO-BASICS APPROACH

ROBERT MILNER

Guilford, Connecticut

Book Design: Cecile Birchler
Jacket Design: Monte Clair Finch

Library of Congress Cataloging-in-Publication Data is available on record.

ISBN: 978-1-932052-25-1

Printed in the United States of America

Ducks Unlimited, Inc.
The mission of Ducks Unlimited is to fulfill the annual life cycle needs of
North American waterfowl by protecting, enhancing, restoring, and managing important wetlands and associated uplands. Since its founding in 1937,
DU has raised more than
$1.3 billion, which has contributed to the conservation of over
9.4 million acres of prime wildlife habitat in all fifty states, each of the
Canadian provinces, and in key areas of Mexico. In the U.S. alone, DU has
helped to conserve over 2 million acres of waterfowl habitat. Some 900
species of wildlife live and flourish on DU projects, including many threat-
ened and endangered species.

ACKNOWLEDGMENTS

Many thanks to:

Major Morty Turner-Cooke. Morty is a true friend and expert British field-trialer who took me to many British trials and shoots. I owe Morty a great debt for the education, as well as for the many doors he opened. The Western world owes Morty and his peers a debt as well. As a second lieutenant in 1940, Morty swam off the beach at Dunkirk to rejoin the British army and do his part as England stood alone against Hitler in the twentieth century's darkest hour.

Bill Meldrum. The Queen's Headkeeper at Sandringham and a world-class dog trainer and expert on breeding selection. Bill greatly aided my education on the power of selective breeding in developing good dogs.

The late **Roy Gonia**. With Roy's guidance and advice, I trained my first great field-trial dog, Toni's Blaine Child, a prodigy that placed in derby stakes, qualifying stakes, and open stakes before he was two years old. After I sold him, Toni's Blaine Child went on to become a finalist in three national titles, a feat attained by very few retrievers.

Ray Hunt, the original "horse whisperer." Ray knows more about gentle training methods than any ten other trainers. I learned from Ray the power of using an animal's natural tendencies instead of force.

Konrad Lorenz. His books on ethology got me interested in the "natural" way to train a dog, and stimulated my interest in learning to look for the basic drivers in behavior. His books also document a lot of inherited behaviors and convey the importance of genetics in animal behavior.

Farley Mowat. His book *Never Cry Wolf* stimulated me to learn more about wolf behavior and to apply the knowledge to dog training.

CALL TO ACTION

The success of Ducks Unlimited hinges upon each member's personal involvement in the conservation of North America's wetlands and waterfowl. You can help Ducks Unlimited meet its conservation goals by volunteering your time, energy, and resources; by participating in our conservation programs; and by encouraging others to do the same. To learn more about how you can make a difference for the ducks, call 1-800-45-DUCKS.

TABLE OF CONTENTS

FOREWORD

It has been almost forty years since Richard A. Wolters introduced his revolutionary dog-training method with the publication of *Gun Dog*, the first of a series of books designed to teach bird hunters how to train their own dogs. The new training technique was based on both science and common sense. The science came from animal behaviorists, who were shedding new light on the ways dogs learn. The common sense, of course, had been around for years, buried under layers of "sage" advice from so-called "expert" trainers. It was up to Wolters—the former rocket scientist who spent his later years proving that you don't need to be a rocket scientist to train hunting dogs—to unearth it.

Like the Wolters' books, this new volume is no small discovery. Its subject, specifically, is how to train retrievers for waterfowling and upland bird hunting. It, too, is based on science and common sense. The science comes from an even better understanding of how dogs learn, as well as new research into canine evolution. The common sense has been around for years, but has gotten buried by field-trial experts whose breeding and training methods run counter to what the average hunter needs in a retriever. This time it is veteran dog trainer Robert Milner who has taken on the task of setting things right, taken a step forward to show hunters how to get back to the basics of retriever training.

In the case of retrievers, a lot more than our understanding of them has changed in the last forty years. According to Milner, the dogs themselves have changed—and not for the better:

"The typical Labrador retriever of thirty or forty years ago was a gentle, calm dog. Today an unfortunately large number of Labradors are hyperactive and difficult to train. The basic reason for this shift appears to be our field-trial system."

During his more than thirty years of training retrievers and judging field trials in the U.S. and England, Milner began noticing some striking differences between retrievers in this country and those on the other side of the pond. A much larger percentage of puppies from American field-trial stock tended to be hyperactive, with a propensity for running off with a stick or ball, a definite precursor to hard-mouth behavior. The great majority of pups from British field-trial stock, however, were calm in nature, with a tendency to return a stick or ball on their first retrieve and deliver it to hand.

This trend became alarming to Milner, who realized that what he and many other professional trainers had been doing—through selective breeding and training—was creating an American retriever that was increasingly "too hot" for the average hunter to handle. As Milner sums it up:

"The gist of all this is that the average hunter is low in dog-training skills, which is as it should be. The community of dog experts should be promoting the selective breeding of a dog that the average hunter can train, and enjoy. We should not be breeding a dog with a bundle of genetically transmitted behavioral tendencies that make him difficult to train into a good working dog. The average hunter should not have to get a Ph.D in dog training in order to come up with a dog that is pleasant to hunt with and pleasant to live with."

In contrast to the heavy-handed tactics of most training programs, this one offers techniques that are good for you and good for your dog. Through gentle training methods learned from Ray Hunt—the original "horse whisperer"—Milner shows you how to train a retriever by using its own natural tendencies instead of force. He also shows you how to pick a retriever with the right genetic make-up, so that you don't choose a high-octane dog that is better suited for field-trialing than for hunting. The result is a calm, steady and obedient companion—at home and in the field.

Chuck Petrie
Executive Editor
Ducks Unlimited magazine

THIS BOOK IS DEDICATED TO MY FATHER, BOB MILNER.
HE TAUGHT ME MORE THAN I EVER KNEW.

CHAPTER 1

THE DUCK HUNT

THE OLD STATION wagon plowed south down Highway 61 through blowing snow. The boy fidgeted with anticipation next to his grandfather, who drove steadily, concentrating on the road ahead. The weather forecast called for a heavy front, with snow approaching from the northwest. The Mississippi River had been above twenty-one feet at Memphis for a week. The old man knew that this would be a day of days for a duck hunter.

Jake, a four-year-old yellow Labrador retriever, lay sprawled across the back seat sleeping, while Smoke, an eighteen-month-old black Lab, turned restlessly in his crate at the back of the car. This was Smoke's first duck hunt, and a rare event for the boy as well. Jake, on the other hand, was a veteran, and it was his arrival whine that made the old man glance right and notice the outline of the Indian mound at the edge of the low beams.

The Indian mound was the old man's signal that the driveway for the Beaver Dam duck club was just two hundred yards ahead. He slowed and squinted through the glare reflecting off the snow, almost feeling his way to the drive, then up it toward the clubhouse. "Leave your dog in the crate so he doesn't make a nuisance of himself," he told the boy when they stopped. "Grab your boots and we'll go in and change."

The old man opened the rear of the car and grabbed his waders. With a "here Jake," he strode toward the front door, followed by his handsome dog. The boy fished around the back seat, got his waders, and hurried after him. Inside, the kitchen overflowed with club members finishing breakfast and organizing the day's shooting. Several dogs roamed around. The old man stood and talked for a few minutes, while Jake sat quietly at his side...in spite of the attentions of two other dogs that were insistently sniffing and poking at him.

"Sam, that dog is too well mannered for an ornery old coot like you," said Chubby, the club patriarch.

"They say dogs take after their masters," the old man replied. "The boy and I will be going up to Round Pond south of Doc's hole, if that's OK with everyone."

"Chuck and I would be glad for y'all to come with us up to Boyd's hole. We killed our limit in a half-hour there yesterday."

"No thanks," said the old man. "We've got Tim's new pup today and he's liable to be short on manners. He'll do much better with less attention."

Walking back to the car, the old man handed Tim a leash and said, "Here, put this lead on Smoke so you can keep him under control. We've spent a lot of time training him to be obedient other places. We need to be especially sure he understands that hunting is a place to mind his manners." As he opened the car door he added, "Put the leash on before you take him out of the crate. You want to be totally sure he's under control."

Tim took the leash and put it on Smoke before taking the dog from the crate in the back of the old station wagon. Then he closed up the back, and the old man pulled down by the boat ramp, turned the car around, and backed the boat trailer down to the water's edge.

"Help me load up the boat before we put it in the water," the old man said, lifting the guns out of the car. "You take Smoke and tie him up to that pole so he'll sit quietly while we're loading up."

Tim tied up Smoke and then put the motor on the square-stern duck boat. Then he fetched the gas tank, decoys, and paddles. The old man handed Tim a life vest, saying, "Put this on and then hold the bowline when I back her into the water." He launched the boat and parked the car.

Getting in the boat, the old man said, "Slip the lead off Smoke and walk him down the bank so he can do his business. Take Jake with you, and pick up ten or fifteen rocks and put them in your pocket. I'll start the motor and let it warm up."

The boy walked the two dogs down the bank, letting them wander about and sniff the bushes within range of his flashlight beam. He stopped long enough to pocket some rocks, then walked back with the dogs to the waiting boat.

Black shadowy forms loomed in the flashlight's glare as they approached the thicket surrounding the pond. The old man cut the motor and paddled through the tightly spaced cypress trees crowding over the boat trail into Round Pond. As they cleared the trees into open water, the old man played the light over a few broken, weathered remnants of two-by-fours nailed to a big, gnarled old cypress stump.

"That was Nash Buckingham's blind back in the heyday of Beaver Dam. The last twenty-five-duck limit from Beaver Dam was shot from that blind on December 30, 1929. The entry is recorded in the club shooting log. In 1930 the limit was lowered to fifteen."

Reaching to the center of the duck hole, the old man handed a sack of decoys to the boy, saying, "Let's get these decoys put out. It's getting close to shooting time."

As the boy started tossing decoys out, Smoke would lunge against his tether with each throw and the boy would yell "Stay!"

"Hold it," exclaimed the old man. "Smoke is not going anywhere with that tether tying him in the boat. Your yelling just gets him more excited, and teaches him that 'stay' means fight and lunge against the leash."

After Tim had tossed out six or eight decoys, Smoke settled down and sat still.

"Now you can tell him 'stay' and he'll get the right association," said the old man. "Stroke him gently on the shoulder and tell him 'good dog' now that he's sitting still like we want."

A little later, Tim noticed Jake stiffen a bit and prick up his ears while staring intently through the low clouds scudding across the dim, gloomy treetops of the gray dawn.

"Get ready," whispered the old man. "Jake hears some ducks in the clouds."

Suddenly four mallards popped out of the gray, snow-flecked mist. Their wings were cupped as they dropped like rocks straight down toward the decoys. The old man's 32-inch Parker dropped two. The boy missed the first shot, but killed one climbing out.

"Quiet your dog down," said the old man. "He needs to learn that the duck boat is a place to sit quietly." Smoke was jerking against the tether in a fruitless effort to launch himself after the downed ducks.

Tim gave him a jerk on the collar and calmly commanded him to sit. Upon compliance, Tim gently stroked him on the shoulders. Jake, who was not tied, looked with great interest at a crippled duck swimming rapidly past the decoys. His look was intense but he sat calmly. "Jake has done this often enough that he knows we're not going to pick up ducks till we are done," the old man said as he raised his gun and shot the one cripple on the water.

Half an hour later they had a limit of four ducks each. The last two killed were floating in open water ten yards past the decoys. "Now we can let Smoke retrieve his first duck," said the old man, gesturing out past the decoys. "Send him for that last one down."

"What about the decoys?" asked Tim.

"Smoke has always found training dummies well past decoys," said the old man. "So he'll go right on through them to the duck. He hasn't learned yet to expect to find anything in the decoys."

Tim unsnapped Smoke's tether and sent him for the duck, which Smoke deftly retrieved. When he got back to the boat, Tim put a hand on his collar to help him in. Then he asked the old man, "What about that duck thirty yards to the left?"

"Send him for that one," said the old man.

Tim sent Smoke, who swam like an arrow straight back to the spot where he'd picked the first duck. Tim blew his whistle, trying to get Smoke to stop for a hand signal. "Save your breath," said the old man. "Wait till Smoke finds out that he doesn't know where the bird is. Then he'll be more prone to take some help from you."

Smoke swam rapidly past the previous duck's resting place, then he started wavering and looking left and right with uncertainty. "Now," said the old man. "Blow the whistle."

Tim blew the whistle and Smoke turned to look at him. Tim gave a hand signal to the left. Smoke swam straight back. "Do it again," ordered the old man.

Tim blew the whistle and Smoke turned again to look at him. Tim gave a hand signal to the left. At the same time, the old man threw a rock that splashed just by the duck. Smoke saw the splash, swam straight to the duck and retrieved it.

After Smoke was back in the boat, the old man said, "Tim, snap that tether back on Smoke. He won't be trustworthy for quite a few hunts yet." Untying the boat he said, "While you are picking up decoys, I'll have Jake retrieve a couple of those ducks from the buck brush where the wind has blown them." They paddled out to the decoys, and Tim began to pick them up and stow them.

The old man sent Jake for a duck. Jake swam thirty yards and turned to look at the old man. He commanded "back" and gave Jake a hand signal to send him on back toward the ducks in the brush. Every twenty yards or so, Jake would look back to the old man for a hand signal. Two more hand signals put Jake into the buck brush, from which he emerged a few minutes later swimming back to the boat with a duck.

"Grandpa," said Tim, "the field-trial folks call that popping, when the dogs looks for a hand signal without being stopped on the whistle. They count it as a fault."

"I count it as intelligent," said the old man. "Every smart dog I've ever had looked to me for directions on a blind retrieve. It is the sign of a smart, cooperative dog. It also cuts down considerably on whistle blasts and noise in the duck blind, which makes duck hunting generally more enjoyable."

The two dogs took turns retrieving the rest of the ducks. Smoke required the help of an occasional rock splash to succeed. After the last duck and decoy were picked up and stowed, the old man directed Tim to snap Smoke once again to the tether, and they headed back across the lake to the clubhouse. The old man guided the boat up to the boat dock and Tim hopped out and made fast the bow. He released Smoke and started for the clubhouse.

"Whoa!" exclaimed the old man. "If you want to train Smoke to be under control, you need to keep him under control. Whatever you allow him to do is what you are training him to do." He handed Tim a leash and said, "Take him with you into the clubhouse, but keep him on the leash until we are through and back in the car. This first hunt is the one that teaches Smoke what you expect from him on hunting trips, so don't operate on hope. Make sure he gets the right picture."

The old man headed up to the clubhouse, with Jake walking easily with him. After he had changed out of waders and written up the morning's hunt in the club journal, the old man relaxed with a cup of coffee in front of the fire, with Jake lying on the floor at his side. He compared notes with Chubby.

"We got a limit of mallards in forty-five minutes," commented Chubby. "How did it go for Tim and the new dog?"

The old man responded, dropping his hand down to stroke Jake's head. "We each got a limit, and they both got a reasonable start."

CHAPTER 2

TRAINING A
GUN DOG IS EASY

TRAINING A GUN DOG IS EASY. All you have to do is educate yourself a little, develop a plan, and follow through with it. The tough part is deciding and defining what you want your dog to be. When you have that picture firmly in mind, the training program unfolds with remarkable ease. Training a gun dog is more a matter of not interfering with Pup's learning processes.

DECIDE WHAT YOU WANT

1. *Obedience* is by far the most desirable trait in a gun dog. After all, an obedient dog, even if he retrieves no ducks, at least doesn't spoil the hunting day. On the other hand, the dog that is out of control is a real pain in the neck, regardless of how many ducks he retrieves.

   Nothing is more unpleasant than spending a morning trapped in a duck blind with an unruly dog and his shouting, ineffective, short-tempered owner. It is much easier, and infinitely more pleasant, to leave the dog at home and retrieve your own ducks.

Obedience is the most treasured trait in a gun dog, and also the most valuable gift you can give your dog. The obedient, well-mannered dog is pleasant to be around. This is good for the dog, good for you, and good for your family. Having a well-mannered dog means you and your family can enjoy his full companionship—anywhere, anytime.

I work in an office, and take my gun dog, Jake, a yellow Lab, to work with me nearly every day. He brings a little extra sunshine into everyone's life. He is always very happy to see his friends at the office, and they are happy to see him. It's amazing how therapeutic it can be to share a moment of companionship with such an open and affectionate friend. Jake has raised morale and productivity tremendously at the office. And on days when he's not there, the atmosphere takes a noticeable downward turn.

Lessons in obedience should start early, and be reinforced throughout a dog's life.

The days just seem better with a dog around. And when you get yourself all wound up in some "crisis" at the office or at home, just reaching down to rub a friendly and grateful head can help put things right again. Your dog can be your greatest stress-reduction strategy. Maybe that's his most valuable gift to you.

Obedience is a great life-enhancing benefit for your dog as well. Look how much more time he gets to spend with you and his human pack. The most valuable time for him is time spent with you, his pack leader. This always reminds me of the old saying that dogs need plenty of space to roam. That is hogwash. The dog has been selectively bred for hundreds of years to socially bond with man. That's where he wants to be, with his master.

The classic example of this is a dog's behavior when his master leaves to go to work.

If a dog is kept in a three-by-four-foot dog crate, he will turn around a couple of times, lie down, and go to sleep, awaiting his master's return. If the dog is kept in a twenty-acre fenced field, he will pick the shady spot closest to the gate, turn around a couple of times, lie down, and go to sleep, awaiting his master's return. The moral: The thing your dog wants most is to be with you. Thus the most valuable gift you can give him is obedience and good manners, so he can spend more time with you.

Obedience may also save your dog's life. Some day you may park next to a busy highway and let the dog out of the car while not paying enough attention to him. You will look up and see him headed for heavy traffic, chasing some wonderful scent with his nose. That's when obedience can pay off handsomely...when you call him and he stops short of the traffic.

2. *Steadiness* is another important quality. Pup should have impeccable manners and steadiness in the duck blind or pheasant field when the birds are falling, flushing—or in

any other tempting situation. This behavior is simply an extension of obedience, and is easy to achieve if you structure your training plan properly.

Pup is not born with good manners such as heeling and sitting. These and other self-control behaviors require the most training.

3. *Energy and persistence in retrieving* is also highly desirable. This behavior is a slam-dunk. Pup is born with the retrieving. All you have to do is a minimum amount of development at the appropriate times in the training plan. The major problem you will have with the retrieving behavior is restraining yourself from giving Pup too much of it.

4. *A proficiency in blind retrieves* makes for a superior gun dog. Then, when you've knocked down a distant bird that the dog didn't see, you can quickly and efficiently direct him to the bird with a minimum amount of noise and activity. This behavior is also quite easy to train and follows very naturally if you start it at the proper time. Timing is most of the battle on this one.

EDUCATE YOURSELF

When you've figured out what you want, educate yourself about how Pup learns and how he communicates. Much of this is covered in chapters 9 and 10. Additionally, you might borrow a basic psychology text and read the parts about animal behavior modification. You might also read a little on how wolves communicate and interact. There are several books on the subject, and they give some remarkably good insights into your retriever's behavioral mechanisms. A little effort spent learning what makes Pup tick will pay off a thousandfold in making the training process easier, and you will wind up with a much better student.

DEVELOP A PLAN

Next, set up some sort of training outline and schedule. Figure out roughly when you want to accomplish the various portions of Pup's training program. Establish realistic goals and objectives and be flexible. If you and your dog are not meeting the schedule, change it to fit your circumstances. You will find that just having the plan will vastly simplify your training program, regardless of the degree of adjustment required.

DON'T TRAIN WHAT YOU HAVE TO UNTRAIN LATER

As you progress with Pup's training program, evaluate his behaviors according to how desirable they are in a gun dog. Human nature is such that we tend to train, promote, or allow behaviors that may be entertaining or easy to ignore. Ask yourself if these behaviors are desirable in a hunting dog. Often they have a very negative value, and require extra training and some degree of punishment to eradicate.

A dog is a creature of habit. Any behavior you encourage, or allow, will start becoming a habit. Evaluate it accordingly. If it doesn't have value in the duck blind, then don't let it occur. Life is a lot more pleasant for Pup if you never let the bad habits start, for then you don't have to resort to punishment to change those bad habits. It is better to nip negative-valued behaviors in the bud.

RECOGNIZE WHICH BEHAVIORS NEED TRAINING

Recognize which behaviors are already there and which need training. This principle applies mainly to retrieving. Your retriever is born with the instinct to chase after an object falling from the sky. He is not born with good manners such as heeling, sitting, staying, coming, etc. Obviously, these self-control behaviors require the most training.

EXECUTE THE TRAINING PLAN

In executing the training plan your guiding principle should be "quality not quantity." You do not have to give Pup a training session every day. However, you must maintain the appropriate relationship all the time. You must be the pack leader all the time. I have trained a couple of my personal gun dogs very nicely with one thirty-minute training session per week.

Along the way, try not to listen to all the "experts." They will interfere with the consistency of your plan.

Develop your plan and execute it according to the commonsense test. If it makes sense, try it. If it doesn't make sense then don't try it. There are no magic tricks to training a dog. A simple, logical training program is very effective for the dog, and very pleasant and enjoyable for the trainer.

CHAPTER 3

FIVE KEY POINTS FOR TRAINING RETRIEVERS

1. OBEDIENCE FIRST

The most common deficiency in the average hunter's gun dog training program is a lack of emphasis on obedience and steadiness.

If I could persuade the average gun dog owner to do *one thing* better as a trainer, it would be to spotlight obedience and emphasize the non-retrieve. The non-retrieve is when Pup sees a bird or dummy fall but doesn't get to retrieve it. The trainer or another dog retrieves it while Pup watches.

Obedience is the most important thing you can teach your retriever.

We took a wrong turn somewhere in the evolution of training, and now go about the retrieving and steadying processes in a totally illogical manner. We take a young dog and give him hundreds of retrieves with no restraint. For the first thousand retrieves, we encourage the dog to take off at will after the falling dummy. Then, after we have him well trained to break, we change the rules and decide to make him steady — which requires a certain amount of punishment to counteract the breaking behavior we have just trained.

The sequence should be reversed. Train him on obedience first, and train him to be steady by teaching him to *expect* to be steady. This is done with non-retrieves.

To develop steadiness, emphasize the non-retrieve. Throw out a dummy or two, then go and pick them up while he watches. You should be picking up 75 percent of what Pup sees fall.

As soon as Pup is proficient at basic obedience, the "stay" drill should include some falling dummies. While he's sitting, toss out a dummy or two. Then go and pick up the dummies while he watches. If you are picking up 75 percent of what Pup sees fall, then Pup doesn't expect to retrieve everything that drops from the sky. He becomes steady, with little effort and no punishment. Additionally, he develops into a calm, pleasant hunting companion. (The same principle applies to the older dog in hunting situations. If you send the dog immediately every time a bird falls, you are training him to break. Make his life easier by making him wait.)

When duck hunting, wait till you have several ducks on the water before you send Pup to retrieve. Unless wind or current is carrying off the ducks, it won't hurt them to float for half an hour. If you are shooting doves, pick up the short, easy ones yourself. Let Pup sit for ten or fifteen minutes before he is sent for the difficult retrieves. The exception of course is the crippled bird, for which you send Pup quickly to reduce the odds of escape.

The practice of delayed retrieving also pays dividends by making it easier for Pup to learn hand signals and blind retrieves. If you have four or five dead ducks on the water that have been there a while, Pup is not going to remember exactly where they are. He knows they are there and will eagerly cast off in their general direction, but his certainty will waver and he will be prone to take some help from you. Conversely, when you engage in the practice of immediately sending Pup on every fall, you are training him in self-reliance. When he's launched on the splash, he knows exactly where that bird is and will quickly pick it up. After he's found several hundred birds all by himself, he is going to be difficult to convince that he needs help from you in the form of hand signals.

2. COMING ON COMMAND
One of the most common obedience problems is failure to come on command.

This is as prevalent in young, green dogs as breaking is in older hunting dogs. Both problems stem from a lack of obedience. If a dog is well trained to heel, sit, stay, and come, he'll do nearly anything you want. The problem lies in the definition of "well trained." A dog is well trained in obedience when he is obedient in the face of any level of distraction. That means he will respond properly when the neighbor's cat walks by, when another dog is playing next to him, and even when shotguns are shooting and ducks are falling.

3. TOO MUCH DOG

The average hunter appears to be "overdogged," or to have a dog that is too hot for him to handle.

I place the blame for this on our field-trial system. Our retriever field trials were brought over from England in the early 1900s, along with the golden and Labrador retrievers. The trials were small and very representative of a day's shooting, and the skills judged were those that had value to the hunting dog and hunter. The trials emphasized game-finding ability, softness of mouth, and calmness of demeanor. The typical Labrador retriever of thirty or forty years ago was a gentle, calm dog. Today an unfortunately large number of Labradors are hyperactive and difficult to train. The basic reason for this shift in breeding selection appears to be our field-trial system.

Unfortunately, our field trials—mainly because of increasing entries—have evolved over the years into elimination contests that evaluate skills that are of little importance in a hunting dog. These behaviors include lining, angle entries into water, pinpoint marking, and precise handling at long distances. Gone by the wayside are line manners and obedience, as well as game-finding initiative. Moreover, training precision lining and long-distance handling requires a great deal of repetition, and some degree of punishment. The dog that excels at these skills tends to be hyperactive, with a high pain threshold, which is exactly the type of dog we are breeding today.

4. ELECTRIC COLLARS

The electric collar, which can create as many problems as it solves, is becoming far too predominant a training tool.

The electric collar is a great training tool in the hands of a good trainer. However, there are astronomically more electric collars than there are good trainers. The truth is: In order to train a dog with the electric collar you must be able to train him without it. The collar does not magically impart to the guy holding the transmitter the knowledge and skills of dog training. Most folks buy an electric collar to solve a basic obedience problem, and generally end up abusing the dog and not solving the problem, or trading one problem for an even bigger one. Proper training can solve nearly all problems in basic obedience, and you don't need an electric collar to do so.

5. SELECTIVE BREEDING

We have forgotten the basic goals of breeding selection and have embarked on a course of producing better dogs by training rather than breeding.

The Labrador is the breed I most commonly work with, and I am alarmed at the trends I see. It has become the general custom to force-fetch train every dog. This corrects any tendency to drop birds, mouth birds, or run off to the bushes with birds. It also masks the genetic tendencies toward those behaviors.

We are now masking with training the major trait that we spent a hundred years developing through selective breeding— namely, delivery to hand with a soft mouth. If we take a hard-mouthed dog and put him through the force-fetch program so that he delivers gently to hand, he will then behave like a great dog. We may even make him a field champion through superior training. However, his puppies will still have that genetic tendency toward hard mouth, and we will be going backwards in the selective-breeding process.

Two other examples of behaviors that have a very significant genetic component that we mask with training are:

Hyperactivity. We train the hyperactive dog to be under control and be a gentleman. The electric collar is quite popular for this. Put a hyperactive dog in the hands of a good trainer with an electric collar and that dog will make an excellent gun dog or field-trial dog, but his puppies will probably inherit the same hyperactivity. His puppies will be just as difficult to train as the sire was.

Cooperative Nature. We generally characterize these dogs as "soft" and tend to give them away as pets when they flunk the electric-collar program. Thus we are tending to remove from the breeding pool dogs that exhibit this valuable trait. This trait of "cooperative nature" is extremely important to the average hunter, because the average hunter is usually quite low in dog-training skills.

The gist of all this is that the average hunter is low in dog-training skills, which is as it should be. The community of dog experts should be promoting the selective breeding of a dog that the average hunter can train, and enjoy. We should not be breeding a dog with a bundle of genetically transmitted behavioral tendencies that make him difficult to train into a good working dog. The average hunter should not have to get a Ph.D. in dog training in order to come up with a dog that is pleasant to hunt with and pleasant to live with.

We probably need to look back to England for solutions. They still have the same field trials they had eighty years ago, still selectively breed for major traits, and still get rid of dogs that lack a cooperative nature and predisposition toward trainability.

I, for one, get my personal dogs from England. They are calm, cooperative, and pleasant to live with, and they find all the birds I shoot. I've gotten lazy and prefer a dog that has gotten most of the required talents through selective breeding.

British field trials still emphasize traits that hunters want in their hunting dogs: game-finding ability, a soft mouth, and a calm demeanor.

CHAPTER 4

THE TOP TEN PRACTICES THAT INTERFERE WITH TRAINING

TRAINING YOUR DOG is extremely easy if you control his environment and channel his behavior in the directions you want. Your dog will practically train himself if you keep from interfering too much. However, many common training practices are totally counterproductive. The major culprits are:

1. RAISING PUP OUTSIDE

The belief that hunting dogs should be raised outside in a pen persists with great tenacity. This belief is hogwash today. It was probably valid fifty or a hundred years ago. Then the kids were outside and spent a lot of time with the puppy during the formative years of both. That way kids and puppies learned to communicate with each other.

Today, however, the situation is different. The kids are all in the house watching TV, playing video games, or cruising the

Internet. Any puppy relegated outside to the pen will grow up in relative isolation, deprived of the social interaction that he needs to develop communication skills, and more important, to develop the bond with people that gives him a desire to please. That desire to please is the basis of a lot of reward-based training. Without it you've made your job much harder.

Pup should be raised in the house. Then he and you both develop the communication skills necessary to make Pup a great gun dog. Additionally, Pup develops the desire to please that enables a lot of reward-based training. Raising Pup in the house makes things easier for both you and him.

2. Giving Pup an Unlimited Diet of Uncontrolled Retrieves

The practice of training Pup to retrieve by throwing him countless out-of-control retrieves is sheer foolishness. Pup is born with the retrieving instinct. His mother gave it to him. And whether you give him one retrieve or ten thousand retrieves, you are not going to improve his genetic inheritance.

© Bill Buckley

You can't improve Pup's drive and retrieving instinct, but you can control it and channel it in the right direction.

I have occasionally seen young dogs that show little interest in retrieving. Sometimes further investigation uncovers the fact that such a pup retrieved wonderfully when he was younger, but suddenly quit. The cause can quite literally be too much retrieving. Thirty or forty retrieves in a row can bring the young pup to the edge of his physical capacity. He is growing at a phenomenal rate, and most of his energy is going toward that growth. Unlimited retrieves can put him in a state of exhaustion and physical pain.

The greatest and most insidious danger of unlimited retrieving is the price it exacts on Pup. You frequently see people throwing untold numbers of balls or training dummies for Pup to retrieve at will. They rationalize this by saying, "I'm developing Pup's retrieving." The real reason they do it is that it is easy and fun for Pup's owner. They don't think of the trouble it will cause Pup later, when they change the rules and want Pup to be steady and under control. They plan to get him steady later.

They are training Pup to be out of control on retrieves. They are training Pup to break, thus ensuring that they will have to use quite a bit of punishment later to train him not to break.

Again, Pup did not inherit obedience and self-control. That's where he needs training, and that's where out-of-control retrieves are totally counterproductive. Pup should have to wait for every retrieve he gets. Then you are training him to wait and to exert some self-control. You are making it easy for him to learn the behaviors you want. You are making it easy to train him without a lot of punishment.

3. REPEATING COMMANDS

Repeating commands is a common mistake people make when dealing with dogs. The practice is an excellent method for training Pup to respond on the third, fourth, or fifth repetition of a command.

Generally, if Pup doesn't respond to the first command, it's not because he didn't hear you. It's because he doesn't feel like responding. The solution is not in repeating the command. The solution is to trigger the response and reinforce your dominance. You should employ a dominance technique such as a direct, threatening stare or "looming over" body position. These techniques are behaviors employed by the pack leader to reinforce dominance in a canine pack.

In obedience classes, I frequently have the handlers go through the obedience drills in silence. That's one of the best ways to counteract the human habit of repeating commands. After all, the dog already knows the responses. He needs the right signal from his master to trigger the response. Silent obedience drills force the handler to speak in Pup's language and produce the right signal.

It takes a little effort to overcome our human nature on the practice of repeating commands, but it pays big dividends. It is much more pleasant to have a dog that responds quickly to the first command. Conversely, it is a pain in the neck to hunt with a dog that responds only when he's constantly bombarded with a steady stream of repeated commands.

4. SHOUTING AT PUP

Yelling usually goes hand in hand with repeating commands. Again, Pup's lack of response is not because he didn't hear you...assuming you've trained him on the required command. It is, rather, because he doesn't feel like responding. If the cause is lack of training, back up and do the training. Otherwise it is a dominance issue and should be corrected now with a mild rebuke rather than waiting until you've firmly trained in the trait of responding only when yelled at. Then it requires a more severe correction.

On a more basic level, shouting only makes it harder for Pup to respond. Shouting usually either excites Pup, or makes him afraid. Neither emotional state makes it easier for Pup to do what you want.

If a 6½-foot NFL linebacker was standing in your back yard yelling—"You better come over here to me, you blankety blank"—would you go to him? Not if you have half a brain. This is approximately the same picture you give your dog when you stand there yelling at him to try and make him come to you. The major difference is that he doesn't understand the words. If your dog is intelligent, he's not going to respond in that situation.

Do yourself and your dog a favor that will make both your lives more pleasant. Don't shout.

5. Pleading When He's Out of Reach

Changing to a pleading tone of voice seems to be another universal human trait triggered by dogs. When the dog gets far enough away that we think he's beyond our control, we revert to an asking tone of voice. You know the one. It has a question mark on the end of the vocalization.

If a dog could speak English, you might as well be saying: "Don't obey me. You are beyond my control." Dogs don't speak English. They speak in the language of tones and mannerisms and body language. They understand very well what that question mark on the end of a vocalization means. That tone signals "don't obey."

Here is where consistency is key in dog training. Always project yourself as if you are in total control. Act the same and use the same tones and mannerisms whether your dog is next to you on a leash or 200 yards away.

6. LETTING PUP "RUN OFF SOME ENERGY"

This is a terrible practice. It will very likely get Pup killed one day, and it trains him to be under control only when he's tired. The very time you most need him under control is when he's brimming with energy and anticipation.

If you regularly let Pup run off energy upon coming out of the house, pen, or car, you are simply training him to be out of control for the first ten minutes around you. Some day you will drive up to a hunting place and park next to a highway. You will let Pup out of the car. He, having been so trained, will be beyond your control for the first couple of minutes as he runs out into the highway in front of an oncoming automobile.

Training Pup to control himself when he's tired is not going to do you much good when he's well rested, fresh, and in the duck blind raring to go. He will lack the self-control necessary to make him a pleasant hunting companion.

7. GIVING PUP TOO MANY MARKED RETRIEVES

Pup gets a marked retrieve every time he sees the bird or dummy fall and thus knows its location. A blind retrieve is when Pup did not see the object fall and must be guided to it by his handler.

The practice of waiting months before starting Pup's hand-signal training is usually justified on the basis of needing to wait till he's older and more mature to start blind retrieves. It is an illogical practice. Old age never made it easier to learn.

This practice falls under the same principle as giving him tons of retrieves and then changing the rules to make him steady. It is making an easy job hard.

The more marked retrieves Pup gets, the more you are training him to find the bird without help from you. The more you do it, the more difficult it is going to be to convince Pup later that you really know where the bird is.

Make both of your lives easy. Start the blind retrieve and hand-signal training on the front end. As soon as he is steady and doing marked retrieves start him on blind retrieves.

8. TESTING INSTEAD OF TRAINING

Many handlers discover anew each day the limits of their dog. They test him to see if he can do what they plan to teach him. A common example is training Pup to do long marked retrieves.

The typical way to teach Pup to do very long marked retrieves is to go out and try it. A helper is sent out 150 yards. He gets out there, shoots, and throws a dummy. You send Pup. Pup goes the distance of the longest retrieve he's had. He starts hunting in a circle at 30 yards and never gets out to the dummy. Now you've taught him to fail.

The right way to do it is:

a. Remember that his longest retrieve was 30 yards.
b. Send the thrower out 150 yards.
c. Walk out with Pup until you are only 30 yards from the thrower.
d. Have the thrower shoot and throw the dummy.
e. Send Pup on the 30-yard retrieve, at which you know he will succeed.
f. Back up 60 yards from the thrower, and have him throw again.
g. Send Pup on this 60-yard retrieve.
h. Continue backing up from the thrower in 45-yard increments until, on the fourth retrieve, Pup is going the full 150 yards.

Structured properly, the lesson is a success, with Pup ending it quite confident on 150-yard retrieves.

Testing Pup to see if he can do what you want is a universal human tendency. It is also universally bad. Always engineer the lesson so that Pup succeeds.

9. Experimenting with Introductions

Introductions to new things are frequently conducted as an experiment to see how Pup reacts. If you are lucky, Pup will react favorably and the introduction will have been successful. If you are unlucky, the introduction will scare the heck out of Pup and you will have a very big problem that may take weeks to solve.

Introductions are often related to the bad practice of testing to train. A classic example is to walk up to Pup and shoot off the

12-gauge to see if he's gun-shy. With this type of introduction, a surprising number of dogs are found to be gun-shy.

The right way to introduce Pup to shooting is to start 150 yards away, watching another dog retrieving. Pup will be very interested. Then a shot is added on each retrieve, while you and Pup still watch from a distance. Then you move closer until, very soon, you are right next to the retrieving performer and Pup is thoroughly enjoying the shooting—because, of course, it is associated with his favorite thing: retrieving.

Why trust to luck? The proper way to train Pup is to engineer the training session to ensure success. Whatever you are introducing Pup to, it is your job to ensure that no unpleasant associations occur.

10. CHANGING THE RULES IN THE HUNTING FIELD

The two major bad practices you see in the field are (a) never using a leash and (b) sending Pup to retrieve the bird while it's still falling.

Many hunters invest hundreds of hours in training their dogs, and then throw away the rules when they get in the field. They forget what a leash is for and let Pup indulge in whatever disobedience he fancies.

They spend hours training Pup to be steady. Then they get in the duck blind and start sending Pup to retrieve while the duck is still falling. After a few repetitions, Pup takes this practice to the next level. He goes without waiting to be sent. Next he progresses to bailing out of the blind at the gunshot.

It makes no difference how much pre-season training you do; when you get to the duck blind Pup is going to give you the amount of obedience and control that you require in that setting.

If you want Pup to be under control in the duck blind, you have to tell him by demonstrating the limits of behavior.

CHAPTER 5

PUP AS A
PACK ANIMAL

THE DYING FIRE CAST dancing shadows on the dark granite of the cave entrance. A hairy, hulking figure squatted near the fire, gnawing at a huge elk quarter. He grew tired and satiated. He tossed the meat to the side and shuffled off into the cave. A few minutes later, a wolf cautiously picked its way toward the discarded prize. The wolf stopped frequently to listen and raise its nose to test the air currents for threatening scents. It snatched the hindquarter with powerful jaws and quickly dragged it off half a mile into the forest, where it was joined by the other members of its pack.

Many generations ago, ancestors of this pack learned that food could be had in proximity to man. Later generations of wolves continued to draw closer to man, especially in times of climatic extremes and difficult hunting.

During this evolving social process, man had been learning as well. An ice age was approaching. Large game was disappearing. Man had to work much harder to kill enough game to survive. Man was also gradually recognizing that the wolves, with their superior sense of smell, could occasionally lead him to the few remaining large animals.

Thus in prehistory arose the social bond between ancestral man and wolves. Note that the relationship was not one-sided, with man saving the wolves. The wolves also had a very beneficial effect on our evolution, allowing the present branch of our family to survive rather than all the other branches that died out. We could have been vastly different creatures...with hulking bodies, knuckles dragging the ground, and a propensity for swinging through the trees. Perhaps we owe a great debt to the ancestors of dogs.

Today we can look to wolf behavior for insights into what makes our dogs tick. That dogs are descended from wolves is no longer mere speculation. Recent DNA analysis has demonstrated that all modern dogs are descended from a single common ancestor, the Eurasian gray wolf. Thus Pup's behavior and communication has its roots in his wolf ancestors. We need to look at wolf behavior to understand our dogs.

DOMINANCE AND SUBORDINATION

The wolf is a pack animal, and the pack gives the wolf its primary underlying behavioral traits—dominance and subordination. All the behavior and communication and order within a wolf pack derive from the powerful instinctive behaviors of dominance and subordination.

There is always a pack leader, and a defined hierarchy of subordination. The pack leader enforces and defends its position in a relatively bloodless manner with several ritual behaviors that act on the instinctive level. These behaviors in order of increasing severity are:

1. **A Direct, Threatening Stare**. A dominant canine gives a steady, direct, threatening stare at an underling to put it in its place. You can see this mechanism in action by going to the zoo and staring steadily into the eyes of one of the lions. It will become very irritated. Similarly, you can stir up a good bit of trouble by trying this on an adult male of our own species in a bar on a Saturday night.

2. **Looming Over**. The dominant wolf stretches up on its toes, raises its hackles, and makes itself appear larger to intimidate a subordinate.

3. **Shoulder Touching**. The dominant wolf puts its muzzle on top of the shoulders of a subordinate. If the desired subordination effect isn't achieved, the dominant wolf will rear up and put its paws on the subordinate's shoulders. This behavior has some very direct relevance to the common problem of dogs jumping up on their owners. If the owner is dominant in the social hierarchy, then the dog is psychologically incapable of jumping up and putting its paws on the owner.

Touching his shoulders gives him a clear signal that you are the dominant member of the pack.

4. **Shaking by the Throat**. When all else fails, the dominant wolf will run at the subordinate, ram it in the shoulder, knock it down, roll it over, grab it by the throat, and shake it roughly while growling fiercely. This extreme behavior is not exhibited with great frequency unless there are two wolves in the pack that are similar in dominance drives. It is also the only dominance demonstration accompanied by a large amount of noise.

Wolves within the pack rarely fight to the point of injury. Usually, when two wolves are similar in dominance drive, they will continue to fight until one leaves the pack. Dominance is determined by individual genetic makeup and enforced by instinctive ritual behaviors.

READING NUANCES OF BEHAVIOR IN PACK MEMBERS
The dominant canine carries itself erect, with ears up, and exhibits a confident manner. It carries its tail high, well above horizontal. The subordinate exhibits a more submissive posture. Reading behavior, posture, and body language of fellow pack members is a highly developed trait and skill in dogs. If the members of a wild pack were not skillful at reading dominance levels and emotional states of fellow pack members, chaos and fighting would predominate, and the pack would not have time to hunt enough game to feed themselves. Therefore, natural selection has made wolves and dogs masters of the skill of reading emotions and posture and body language. Thousands of years of evolution have developed Pup into a creature that can read you like a book. You must be a skillful actor to fool him.

IMPACT OF PACK STRUCTURE ON PUP'S EMOTIONAL STATE

Your dog's mental health depends to a large degree on leadership and consistency. Pup is a product of thousands of years of evolution as a pack animal. He needs a pack leader. If he doesn't get one, he is quite likely to be neurotic. Additionally, he needs a fairly stable position in the pack. You as the pack leader have a responsibility to conduct yourself like the pack leader so that Pup can feel confident of his position. Mixed signals and alternating between leading and following make a dog neurotic.

IMPACT OF PACK DYNAMICS ON TRAINING

Now that you have a basic understanding of the powerful pack behavioral mechanisms that affect Pup, how do you use them in training?

1. Raise Pup in the house so that he imprints with the right pack. Raising him in the house ensures that he associates you as a pack member, as opposed to, say, the neighbor's beagle. Additionally, raising Pup in the house will help develop a bond that becomes a desire to please on Pup's part. Most important, if you and Pup live in the house together, you will both develop communication skills. You will learn how to better communicate with each other.

2. Be quiet. Conduct your training sessions with minimum verbiage. Remember that the dominance mechanisms involve little in the way of sound. Remember also that dogs communicate very little to each other with audible signals.

Most dogs communicate through visual signals provided by motion, posture, attitude, and other aspects of body language.

3. Be the pack leader. This means acting with authority when you expect Pup to obey. It means conducting yourself with authority in training sessions and when hunting. Your behavior is the only way Pup can tell whether it is work time or play time. Have a signal for play time. When it is work time, don't send play signals with your voice or mannerisms. Be consistent and don't give mixed signals. Don't change your tone of voice or body language just because Pup happens to be 300 yards away, or just because he's not wearing that check cord. Always act like the pack leader when you want a response from Pup, because he reads you like a book.

Start the obedience properly. Train Pup to heel and to watch you. When you do the quick turns and direction changes, impart enough momentum so that you lift his front feet off the ground. This is of major importance in the initial formation of dominance.

Give a lot of your reward petting as slow stroking on top of Pup's shoulders to reinforce your dominance in a positive manner. Pay attention to Pup's attitude. When his tail is up high and his ears are up, he's a lot less likely to be responsive to you. He should show his tail at or below horizontal, and his ears should be slightly back. Then Pup is properly submissive and will respond consistently.

4. When you must punish, use canine mechanisms. For minor infractions, and as a first resort, use a direct, threatening stare. For a more serious rebellion, grab Pup by the nape of the neck and give him a shake with sufficient vigor to pick up his front feet. If he is really bad, and if you are strong enough, pick him up by the nape of his neck and the loose

skin above his rear quarters and give him a shake so that all four of his feet are off the ground.

CHAPTER **6**

LEARNING TO
SPEAK "DOG"

AS I MENTIONED in the last chapter, Pup doesn't speak English; he speaks "wolf," or "dog," a language that you will recognize. It is mostly sign language—read with the eyes, not heard with the ears. If you watch a pack of dogs or a pack of wolves, you will hear very little in the way of sound. Most of the social interaction is visual. Communication consists of reading body language, attitude, posture, and mood. Thus the dog's most important organ for communication is the eye, not the ear or the voice. The silent trainer is generally much more effective.

One of the greatest obstacles to successful dog training is the human voice. We humans have a great deal of trouble keeping our mouths shut. All that sound means mainly excitement or aggression to a dog. Either emotional state makes it more difficult for the dog to perform the behavior you are trying to establish.

❖

SILENCE IS GOLDEN

One of the most important things a novice trainer with a young dog can do is keep his mouth shut. Again, dogs communicate with vision, not with sounds and hearing. They read posture, attitude, expression, and body language.

At the start of training, commands mean nothing to a dog. The command acquires meaning only after being paired with a response. Almost universally you will see people doing it backwards and giving the command while the dog is doing everything but the desired behavior. They think the command is going to elicit the behavior, and they are wrong. The command will elicit the behavior only after it has been paired with the appropriate behavior for a number of times and the sequence has been rewarded.

Some years ago I learned by necessity that dogs respond more readily when the trainer keeps his mouth shut. I had throat cancer. Several rounds of surgery and some radiation rendered me unable to speak above a whisper for a period of about six months. Obviously, I had to train dogs without my voice. To my surprise, I discovered that dogs learn much more readily when the trainer uses his voice very sparingly, and mainly as a reward. Desired behavior is learned much more rapidly when initially paired with a visual signal, such as a raised hand to signal stay, a step back with a dropping of the shoulder to signal come, etc. The verbal command is added later, as a substitute for the visual signal.

When you analyze a typical training session, it becomes obvious that the trainer instinctively knows the right signal to give. Take the command "sit." If you require the trainer to be silent, most will automatically move their hand back over Pup's head so that he has to look up to follow the hand. This, in conjunction with light upward pressure from the choke collar, will usually cause him to sit.

Dogs respond more readily to visual signals than to verbal ones. They are also experts at reading attitude, body language, and mood. Be aware of the signals you are sending, and be consistent.

Similarly, when they want him to stay and can't give a verbal command, most people will raise their hand in a traffic cop's "stop" gesture as they step away from Pup.

The amazing thing is that most people will automatically pick these signals. They know, at least on an instinctive level, how to communicate with Pup. The moral here is that if you keep your mouth shut during initial training, you instinctively know the right signals to use.

When you're training Pup on obedience, try some silent drills. You'll be pleasantly surprised at how well you communicate without your voice. You will find that Pup usually learns more quickly with a visual signal than with noise.

SINS OF THE VOICE

Generally, a person training a dog uses his voice entirely too much and tends to communicate alarm, aggression, or excitement. None of these emotional states is conducive to successful behavior modification. Here are the most common sins of the voice:

1. **Wrong Association.** The trainer pairs the voice command with other than the desired behavior. This is commonly seen with heeling, when the trainer is saying "Heel! Heel! Heel!" while the dog is every place but in the heel position. This practice just makes it more difficult for Pup to learn the meaning of heel. If you only say the command "heel" when Pup is in the heel position, walking alertly at your left or right knee, then Pup will very quickly learn the meaning of the command. Dogs learn a command by associating that command with a particular behavior. The command does not cause the behavior until the conditioning process is complete.

2. **Repeating Commands**. When Pup does not respond to a command, it is usually not because he didn't hear it. Repeating the command simply trains Pup to respond to the third, fourth, or fifth command. A lack of response is a common phenomenon when your dominance is flagging. Pup is programmed to periodically test your dominance. When you are sending the wrong signals and not maintaining your position as pack leader, Pup is going to become much less responsive. The solution is not to repeat the commands. The solution is to reinforce your dominance with the appropriate mechanism, such as putting the lead on and doing a heel drill, giving Pup a direct, threatening stare, or shaking him by the neck.

3. **Shouting**. Shouting is frequently seen at dog-training sessions. Shouting is totally counterproductive for dog training. Shouting generally just scares Pup or makes him excited. Neither emotional state is conducive to making Pup more responsive to whatever command he is failing to execute.

4. **Praising Everything**. Some people praise everything that Pup does. When you praise all behaviors, then you deprive yourself of praise as a primary training tool. Use praise sparingly and use it to reward the behaviors that you value. Also, remember that Pup perceives praise by tone and inflection, not by deciphering the words. When Pup is doing something you want him to do, such as sitting quietly in the face of temptation, praise him. When he is doing something undesirable, such as pulling you down the street on the leash, don't sing "heel, heel, heel" to him in a friendly voice. Let him know by your firm, authoritative tone that he is not doing the right thing.

5. **Praising Too Profusely**. Praising Pup too enthusiastically and too much will tend to excite Pup and elevate his emotional state. It tends to make him hyper. That is not the emotional state that you want in a gun dog—therefore, keep it moderate.

Praising Pup too much and too enthusiastically will also signal to Pup that he is the pack leader. In a pack structure, the subordinates usually tease to initiate play with the pack leader. Overindulgence in praise will frequently send signals to Pup that you are subordinate. Those signals make it difficult for Pup to maintain a high level of responsiveness to your commands.

Generally, praise should consist of two or three repetitions of "good dog," which may be accompanied by two or three gentle downward strokes on the top of Pup's shoulders.

ALL THE WORLD'S A STAGE

Communication works both ways. While you are reading Pup, Pup is reading you. Remember that thousands of years of breeding selection have developed Pup into a consummate reader of attitude, emotion, body language, mood, etc. That's how wolf packs survive and keep from degenerating into continual brawls. Thus Pup is well aware of how your day went when you come home in the afternoon. He is also probably aware of whether you are going to be strict or lax in a particular training session. If you want consistent, predictable responses from Pup, you should give him consistent signals on the behavior standards you expect. This means that you must be consistently authoritative, and it means that you must be consistent in the standards of response you require.

You will give Pup a great deal of emotional security by consistently maintaining your position as pack leader, and by giving Pup the signals he expects from a pack leader. When Pup is exhibiting what we interpret as misbehavior and rebellion, such is generally not the case. Disobedience and rebellion are often the result of the trainer giving the wrong signals or the trainer giving mixed signals. Here are a few examples of common transgressions:

1. When Pup is out of reach, you change your tone of voice from authoritative to questioning. This usually occurs at seventy-five feet when Pup is wearing a fifty-foot check cord; or when he is on the other side of a pond; or when, if you're training with an electric collar, you have the dummy collar on him. When Pup goes out of control under such circumstances, it is not because he knows the length of the check cord or because he knows that the electric collar is not on. Pup goes out of control because the trainer has changed his voice. That tone change sends a signal to Pup that the trainer is no longer dominant. Pup reacts accordingly and quits being responsive. Trainer behavior is the real reason that electric-collared dogs get less responsive when they are not wearing the collar.

2. When you are alone with Pup, you are consistently authoritative. When you are in the company of others, you get self-conscious and get more tentative in your tone of voice and mannerisms. Pup tends to read that as a sign of submission and becomes less responsive.

3. When you're training, you're consistently authoritative and do quite well with Pup. When hunting season arrives, you take Pup out and promptly forget most of the rules. You get excited, communicate that to Pup, and don't require the

degree of obedience that you do in training. He starts out with a few minor transgressions, which you ignore. He gets progressively less responsive, until he surpasses your limit of tolerance. You lose your temper and punish him. This sequence can be avoided by maintaining the same standards in both hunting and training.

CHAPTER 7

INHERITED VERSUS LEARNED BEHAVIOR

A DOG IS A PRODUCT of myriad behaviors and reactions. Some of these behaviors are inherited and some are learned. To make a reasonable choice in selecting a puppy, you'll need some guidelines as to which behaviors are inherited and which are learned. This information will help you select parents that display the best set of inherited behaviors, which in turn will increase your the odds of obtaining a puppy that fits your requirements, as well as your level of dog-training skills.

INHERITED BEHAVIORS

Over the years, I have had the wonderful opportunity to observe the behavior of a large number of dogs, as well as the behavior of quite a few of their offspring, of several generations. These observations have left me with some firm convictions on inherited behaviors. I have many times seen a certain strong behavioral tendency in a particular dog, and I have

seen that same tendency transmitted through several generations of its progeny.

Dogs come in all flavors, with a wide variety of behavioral
traits. All dogs are different. I usually explain these differences
in terms of the strength or weakness of a few inherited traits.

1. **Retrieving Desire**. The response of chasing a falling or
   fleeing object is instinctive. A typical puppy will automatically chase a thrown ball or stick. He may not bring it
   back, but he will generally chase it if he sees it. Note that
   he must see it. Some puppies may not develop the eye-
   muscle patterns to track a rapidly moving object until they
   are at least ten or twelve weeks old. Make sure Pup is
   tracking the ball with his eyes before you decide he doesn't
   have retrieving instinct.

**Retrieving desire is something Pup is born with. Toss an object
and he will automatically chase it.**

A respectable degree of retrieving desire is a definite requirement in a good gun dog, but there is such a thing as too much drive. In the field-trial breeding pool over the past twenty or thirty years, we have been breeding an increasing number of dogs with too much go-power and retrieving desire.

As field trials have evolved over the past fifty years, they have become largely a test of lining behavior. To train field-trial-caliber lining behavior requires a great deal of repetition and some amount of pressure in the form of correction. The dogs that are superior candidates for this type of training tend to have an excessive amount of retrieving desire and tend to be hyperactive.

2. **Delivery to Hand**. Some puppies have plenty of instinct to chase a falling or fleeing object but are short on the behavior of bringing it back. This delivery-to-hand trait appears to also have a strong inherited influence. Some puppies seem to have a strong tendency to bring back the retrieve. Others have a tendency to grab the retrieved object and run away with it.

Delivery to hand is another genetically transmitted trait that has great value to hunters and field-trialers. The latter, however, choose to get it through force training rather than breeding.

I have had the opportunity to observe a large number of puppies bred from American field-trial stock, and also a large number of puppies from British field-trial stock. Of the puppies I have observed from British field-trial breeding, 95 percent automatically return with the stick or ball on their first retrieve and deliver it to hand.

Puppies from American field-trial stock are much less prone to bring it back. I would estimate that 30 to 40 percent of American puppies have a tendency to run off with the stick or ball. This trait is the precursor to hard-mouth behavior. Running away to the bush with the prey is what a wild dog does just prior to eating it. I would expect most of these nondeliverers to have a tendency toward hard mouth when they get on birds.

3. **Soft Mouth vs. Hard Mouth**. We have been selectively breeding sporting dogs to develop a soft mouth for hundreds of years. Most dog folks will agree that soft mouth is a genetically transmitted trait. Our training practices in American field-trial circles have reversed that breeding process.

It is now standard practice to force-fetch train nearly every field-trial dog. This conditioning process is a necessary precursor to the process of forcing dogs to develop lining skills. We are producing some great lining dogs with these training practices, but the force-fetch training process also compensates for hard mouth. Thus we are no longer selectively breeding for soft mouth in the field-trial populations.

4. **Swimming**. Swimming is an inherited, instinctive behavior. You can take any litter of puppies that is seven or eight weeks old, entice them into the water, and they will swim automatically and never miss a stroke. A few puppies, if they miss this introduction at seven or eight weeks, will have trouble later in triggering that swimming instinct.

The swimming instinct can be triggered by enticing Pup into the water when he's seven or eight weeks old. If you wait much longer, you may have trouble triggering this natural impulse.

5. **Pointing**. Many retrievers show a definite pointing response. This is a remnant of the crouch-before-pouncing hunting technique displayed by their wild ancestors. This "pointing" is generally elicited by a tight-holding live bird. The dog generally has to be within one or two feet of the bird for the point response to be triggered. The dog will freeze only for a second or two, and will pounce on the bird. To get him to hold the "point" for a longer period, you have to train him to stay standing in position.

I don't, however, think that pointing has any value for a retriever in the upland game or pheasant field. A retriever is a flusher, not a pointer. If you keep Pup under control and within fifteen yards of you, you will get a shot at nearly every bird in your path. Introducing pointing into the equation just makes a simple task difficult.

6. **Calm vs. Hyperactive**. Hyperactivity is a trait that demonstrates how selective breeding for success in American field trials has made a dramatic change in the typical dog. Ask any field-trialer what kind of dog he wants and he will tell you, "A hard-charging dog." We have bred this trait to excess in the field-trial gene pool. Far too high a percentage of dogs in the field-trial population are hyperactive. In an outdoor kennel they tend to pace incessantly. In a backyard they dig holes, chew trees, pull up shrubbery, etc. When you take them in the house they display similar behavior. A hyperactive dog is not pleasant to live with, and is very difficult for the average hunter to train. Conversely, a calm dog is a pleasure to live with and is easy for the average hunter to train.

7. **Pain Threshold or Toughness**. Toughness is another trait that has been highly valued by field-trialers for the past twenty or thirty years. A tough dog is one that takes correction well and bounces back, one that handles the electric collar well. He also tends to be a dog that does not respond well to more gentle training methods. The tough dog is less cooperative and requires more force to train.

   The increasing popularity and use of the electric collar is skewing breeding selection toward this type of dog, especially in the field-trial gene pool. A good trainer can take a tough, uncooperative dog and put him through an electric-collar training program and make a well-mannered gentleman out of him. The problem is that the electric-collar program doesn't change his genes.

   If you saw this dog at a field trial or in training you might say, "That's a very good dog; I think I'll breed him to my bitch." You then arrange for the breeding, and subsequently a litter of puppies arrives. Unfortunately, the puppies are going to be like their parents. That tough, uncooperative male will produce tough, uncooperative puppies— puppies that will need a good trainer and an electric-collar training program.

8. **Game-seeking Initiative**. Game-seeking initiative is measured in how many birds the dog finds. Some people say that a dog with this trait "has a good nose." However, this behavior encompasses far more than having a good nose. The dog that possesses good game-seeking initiative not only has a good nose but knows where to use it. Such a dog will tend to hunt the places where birds are likely to be found. This dog will hunt edges, ditches, cover changes, and shorelines. This is a behavior that some dogs are born with and some aren't.

Game-seeking initiative is an extremely desirable trait in a gun dog. The gun dog that instinctively hunts the edges, ditches, shorelines, and birdy places will flush a lot more birds for the hunter. Additionally, he will more readily dig out the crippled birds on either land or water. The value to the hunter is obvious.

Game-seeking initiative is a very bad trait in a field-trial dog. To win field trials a dog must consistently take a straight line through cover changes, ditches, edges, and shorelines. In fact, you will find that field-trial judges consistently engineer tests so that dogs with a tendency to veer off line at cover changes and shorelines will do poorly. For field trials, you want a dog that punches right through cover changes, ditches, and shorelines with no tendency to hunt.

9. **Nose Users**. Some dogs tend to use their nose more and some tend to use their eyes more to locate game and prey. The nose user has great value to the hunter. When you nick a duck that sails off 200 yards and swims into thick, flooded buck brush, it will take a nose-using dog to dig it out.

The dog must swim the 200 yards and then scout the edge of the buck brush to detect the traces of scent left where the duck swam into the brush. He then has to track that duck through the water, relying on the minute amounts of scent hanging on the brush. This job takes a confirmed nose user.

On the other hand, the nose user is a liability to a field-trialer. In a field trial, a test is set up and all the dogs are run on the same test. Thus you might have a triple marked retrieve in which sixty or more dogs are run. All those dogs are leaving their scent and bird scent on the grass and brush as they make the retrieves. After the first ten or twelve dogs, there is a tremendous amount of scent strewn about the field. A nose-using dog will become confused quickly in these conditions.

10. **Eye Users**. The eye user is the reverse of the nose user. The eye user has great value to a field-trialer, less to a hunter. The eye user tends to be the pinpoint marker that "steps on" a marked retrieve at 200 yards. He is not distracted by his nose on the way to the bird. This trait has great value in field trials, where pinpoint marking is highly rewarded, and where there are oceans of scent to distract a dog that is less sure of the bird's location.

For the hunter, the eye user has less value. It's great if he pinpoints the bird 200 yards out, but conditions frequently prevent a clear view, or the bird swims or runs off from the landing spot. Then the eye user is at a disadvantage. The nose user will probably take a more meandering route to the fall, but he is far more likely to find the bird's scent trail and track it down. The eye user will have a lot more trouble and a lot less success when he misses that pinpoint mark and needs to use his nose to dig out the bird.

11. **Dominance vs. Subordination**. Dominance is a fundamental behavioral trait in all dogs, male and female. It flavors and influences a lot of their other traits and behaviors. Individual dogs are born with some degree of dominance. Obviously, the dog with the highest drive to dominate is the one that becomes the pack leader. The dog with the higher dominance drive is also the one that is more difficult to train. The dominant dog checks more frequently to see if the trainer is still the pack leader. The dominant dog usually requires more force and pressure to train. The dominant-natured dog is generally the preferred type as a candidate for field-trial training.

    The dog with less dominance and more subordination is much easier for the novice dog trainer to handle. The subordinate-natured dog is easily corrected with the raised voice. The subordinate-natured dog works much harder at reading the trainer and tries harder to cooperate. The subordinate-natured dog is by far the best choice for the average hunter.

12. **Tractability**. This trait could also be described as a dog's desire to please. Tractability appears to be closely linked to subordination. There seems to be a much higher percentage of subordinate-natured dogs that are high in tractability. You see the occasional dominant dog that is high in tractability, but the number is small. By definition, a tractable dog is much more desirable as a candidate for training.

❖

LEARNED BEHAVIORS

To get the best puppy, you select the parents with the best mix of inherited behaviors. The puppy will approximate the parents in behavioral traits. Then you train him in the behaviors that you want, according to what his function will be. If Pup is going to be a hunting dog, his training requirements will differ greatly from those of a prospective field-trial dog.

The main learned behaviors are:

1. **Obedience**. Obedience is basically heeling, sitting, and staying. Obedience is an extremely important behavior in a hunting dog. A disobedient dog makes hunting unpleasant, even if he retrieves all the birds. Conversely, an obedient dog is a pleasure to hunt with even if he is not the world's greatest retriever. Proficiency in obedience is measured by the level of distraction he can handle and still maintain his self-control. Your dog is truly obedient when you can walk through a cornfield flushing pheasants every five or ten yards and he stays within fifteen yards, comes to heel when called, and sits when told.

2. **Steadiness**. Your dog is truly steady when he can sit still as you and your hunting buddy light a flock of 100 mallards, flush them, and shoot four or five ducks as they climb out. Then your buddy sends his dog on the first retrieve. If your dog is still sitting calmly, then he is steady.

   The unsteady dog is a liability to you and to himself. The unsteady dog is the one that breaks to retrieve while the bird is still falling. He progresses to breaking every time you shoot...then to breaking when he hears the safety being switched off before you shoot. However, this last behavior doesn't last very long. The unsteady dog puts himself out in the blast cone of the shotgun often

Steadiness doesn't come naturally. You must train Pup to be steady...in all situations.

enough to be deafened at a very young age. After a season or two of hunting, the unsteady dog probably cannot hear a safety click anymore. He will have lost his hearing to shotgun blast.

The unsteady dog also is likely to have his career come to an early end. Breaking and putting himself out in front of the guns is a good way to get shot. Thus steadiness is a very valuable behavior in a hunting dog.

3. **Lining**. Lining has great value for a field-trial dog. A good lining dog will consistently win field trials. Lining is the ability to line a dog up on blind retrieves and send him out on a line when he has seen nothing fall. To win field trials the dog must be capable of taking that line within five to ten degrees of a given direction. That is very fine lining and requires a tremendous amount of training to achieve.

For a hunting dog, however, lining has little value. The hunting dog will be most productive when he hunts where the bird is likely to be. In a hunting situation, when a duck or pheasant is knocked down, the hunter often doesn't know exactly where it fell. Additionally, if the bird is still alive, it is not going to stay where it fell. The productive hunting dog will head out in the general direction he is sent, but will check promising pieces of cover as he ventures out in search of the bird.

In contrast, a lining dog will charge out in an unerring line, regardless of what tempting chunks of cover are off to the left or right. The lining dog has much poorer odds of coming up with the bird in a hunting situation. If you are training a field-trial dog, spend a whole lot of time and emphasis on lining. If you are training a hunting dog, you only need the dog to go out in the general direction he's sent. You don't need a great deal of precision. The hunting dog will be more productive when he goes off in the general direction indicated and checks promising pieces of cover on the way out.

4. **Whistle Stopping and Hand Signals**. For blind retrieves you need to send the dog out after an unseen fallen bird, and you also need to be able to correct his course or "steer" him on the way out to the fall. Stopping on the whistle to turn and look at you is the prerequisite to following hand signals. The dog has to see the hand signal in order to respond to it.

In field trials, judges typically score a dog down for popping, or turning to look for a hand signal when the handler has not blown the whistle to signal the dog to stop and look. Popping is undesirable for a field-trial dog.

For the hunting dog, popping is a plus. A dog that stops and looks to me for a hand signal every twenty yards or so is ideal. I can send that dog on a blind and know I won't have to fight to get him to stop. Popping is a sign of intelligence. The dog understands that he is on a blind retrieve

Learning to read hand signals is a must for the hunting retriever, as he will have to rely on directions from you when he doesn't see the bird fall.

and is cooperating by looking to me for the next hand signal. The blind retrieve can be accomplished quickly, efficiently, and in total silence. That is by far the best performance for a hunting situation.

5. **Staying in the Water**. Staying in the water is by far the biggest difference in field-trial performance and hunting dog performance. Field-trial dogs that stay in the water win field trials. Hunting dogs that stay in the water die of hypothermia.

   Staying in the water can be defined by looking at a fairly common field-trial test and standard field-trial training scenario. Imagine a long, narrow pond that is 50 feet wide and 400 feet long. The dog is run from one end and the bird falls at the other end. A field-trial dog that has been properly trained jumps immediately into the water, swims the 400-foot length of the pond to get the bird, and returns swimming the 400-foot length of the pond. He will swim 800 feet.

A dog that has not been trained to stay in the water will simply run around the water and down the bank, jump in to retrieve the bird, and run back on the bank. He will swim a total of 20 feet.

Now suppose we have the same pond and same retrieve with a few variations. Suppose the water temperature is forty degrees Fahrenheit, the air temperature twenty-eight degrees, the wind blowing twenty knots and spitting snow. Also suppose that there are ten ducks to be retrieved at the end of the pond. The bank runner will make those ten retrieves fairly quickly and be warmer from the exercise

The water-trained dog might swim all the way for all ten ducks, but that's unlikely. It is more likely that he will succumb to hypothermia before he gets past the fifth duck. The moral of the story is that staying in the water not only has a negative value for a hunting dog, the behavior is downright dangerous.

❖

CHAPTER **8**

HOW TO FIND A
GOOD DOG

TO GET A GOOD hunting dog prospect you should do a little investigation prior to the acquisition. As the Labrador retriever is the most popular breed, I will use it as an example. However, the same principles apply to the other retrieving breeds.

© Gary Kramer

Getting a good Lab requires a lot more than simply going out and buying a registered Labrador puppy. Unfortunately, Lab breeding selection has taken several twists and turns during the past fifty years. We now have several Lab gene pools in the U.S., and none of these is selectively breeding for a better hunting dog. These gene pools are:

Field Trials. There is an excellent breeding selection process in the field-trial segment of Labradors. Breeders have made great progress in reducing probabilities of severe hip dysplasia. They have made enormous progress in reducing the incidence of progressive retinal atrophy. Breeders are also producing great field-trial prospects. Field-trial excellence is denoted on pedigrees by the titles FC and AFC, or Field Champion and Amateur Field Champion. A puppy with plenty of these titles in his ancestry will probably be a good field-trial prospect.

However, he may not be a great hunting dog prospect. Over the past fifty years, field-trial behaviors have diverged greatly from hunting behaviors. A puppy that is ideal as a field-trial prospect may be less suitable as a hunting dog prospect. That field-trial puppy has a relatively high probability of being hyperactive, tough, and less tractable. That field-trial puppy will likely require a higher degree of dog-training skills than those possessed by the average hunter.

Hunting Retriever Tests. Hunting retriever competitions arose in the 1980s as a response to hunters' dissatisfaction with the highly regimented and specialized field-trial system. Hunting retriever competitions are pass/fail, with no awards given for first, second, third place, or the like. Hunting retriever competitions were a welcome addition to the retriever world because they recognized that something was wrong with field trials. They recognized that field trials were not the best way to test hunting dogs.

Hunting retriever competitions are great because they give the hunter a venue where he can successfully test his dog. However, these competitions are woefully short in providing breeding selection for better hunting dogs.

Go to nearly any hunting retriever test and you will see the judges setting up contests that evaluate the same behaviors as field trials. The tests are built on the same principles as field trials but are not as extreme or as difficult. Hunting retriever competitions do not test steadiness to a level required for hunting dogs. Rather, they evaluate and place value on lining and staying in the water.

Bench Shows.

Bench shows evaluate a dog's appearance and do not test any behaviors connected with hunting. A strong bench champion pedigree will have a lot of champion (CH) titles in the ancestry. A strong bench pedigree will give you a high probability that a pup will be very handsome. The strong bench pedigree gives you no selection for hunting dog performance traits.

All the titles and pedigrees in the world won't tell you if a particular pup will make a good hunting dog. For that, you'll need to learn about his parents.

THE HUNTING DOG PROSPECT

If you want a good gun dog prospect, there is no title on the pedigree to guide you. You will have to rely on personal knowledge or an inspection of the parents. Since puppies tend to approximate their parents in behavioral traits, look to the parents for the behavioral traits you want in a hunting dog. Go look at the parents. Have the owners work the dogs for you. Ideally, you should go hunting with the owners and the parent dogs. Look for these following traits from the previous chapter:

1. **Retrieving Desire.** Do the parents have a reasonable degree of retrieving desire? They should love it, but not to an extreme. If they look like they would charge through a brick wall to retrieve, they might be too high-strung to make a good hunting dog. Remember that you have to train them.

2. **Delivery to Hand.** Ideally, you would like to pick a pup from parents that automatically deliver to hand and have never been force-fetch trained. If the behavior was in the parents, then the puppies will probably have it. Ask the owner.

3. **Soft Mouth.** You would like to see your pup's prospective parents deliver a bird tenderly to hand. Again, you are ahead of the game if the parents were born with the trait of soft mouth and never had to be force-fetch trained. After all, this is the primary trait we've been selectively breeding retrievers for since we started shooting birds.

4. **Calm Nature.** Observe the parents in working and nonworking environments. If they live in the house and are calm, that is what you want to see. If they live in the kennel, ask why. If they live in the kennel and run or pace constantly, then you don't have to ask. They are no doubt hyperactive and will tend to pass this trait on to their puppies.

5. **Pain Threshold or Toughness.** Observe the handler and dog at a working session. If the handler hauls out the whips and chains and electric collars, this is probably a pretty tough candidate, not the ideal sire for a good hunting dog. If you want a puppy that is easy to train, get one from relatively soft parents.

6. **Game-seeking Ability.** Game-seeking ability is of great importance in a hunting dog and is impossible to determine without going hunting with the dog. You might try to get the owner to run the dog on a couple of long blind retrieves in a place with plenty of cover changes and thickets. If the dog shows an inclination to want to hunt cover and edges, then he's probably high in game-seeking ability—a trait he has no doubt passed on to his pups. In the absence of a hunting trip, you will probably have to rely on the owner's opinion.

7. **Propensity to Use Nose**. The nose user is also extremely difficult to evaluate unless you go hunting with him. Note: It is a bit unreasonable to try to schedule a hunt with the sire and dam of every litter from which you might choose a pup.

8. **Dominance.** Have the owner work the dog. If the dog is bouncing around with his tail high, and his attention focused everywhere but on the handler, then he is showing more dominance than is desirable. The dominant-natured dog usually will not demonstrate maximum cooperation. The more subordinate dog will be carrying his tail lower, will have more attention focused on the handler, and will be more responsive to commands. The more subordinate dog is much more desirable as a parent for your hunting dog.

9. **Tractability**. During the working session, listen to the noise levels. If there is a lot of shouting and repetition of commands, the dog is obviously not great in the tractability department. If he's wearing an electric collar, the same is probably true. Try to find a pup from parents that were easy to train. That greatly increases the odds of your puppy being easy to train.

CHAPTER 9

HOW PUP LEARNS

PUP DOESN'T SIT because you say "sit." He sits because he's been put through a repetitive regimen of behavior conditioning. Pup learns behaviors the same way people learn physical skills like bike riding, tennis, or golf. He learns—usually in spite of the trainer—that the word "sit" followed by his response of sitting produces a reward.

SHAPING BEHAVIOR WITH REWARD
To train Pup effectively you need a basic understanding of animal behavior modification principles. These are fairly simple and fairly familiar, since we humans react along the same lines as animals. The two fundamental principles that apply to canine behavior modification are:

1. Behaviors are formed and shaped by reward.
2. Behaviors are extinguished by lack of reward and by punishment.

The foundation of any good training program should be based on building and shaping desirable behavior by reward training. The key principal here is that a behavior followed by a reward tends to be repeated.

Just about everyone is familiar with the name Pavlov, the Russian physiologist who discovered—about a hundred years ago—that dogs could be trained to salivate at the sound of a ringing bell. Pavlov set up a trial in which he regularly rang a bell before feeding the dogs. After a number of repetitions, the dogs would salivate merely upon the ringing of the bell, without the presence of food. The bell had become the stimulus, or signal, while the salivation was the conditioned response. This has become known as Pavlovian, or classical, conditioning. The key is the sequence:

SIGNAL	RESPONSE	REWARD
bell	salivate	food

After a number of repetitions to establish the signal, the food can be removed from the sequence, and the bell will produce salivation, as diagrammed below:

SIGNAL	RESPONSE
bell	salivate

TRAINING A YOUNG PUPPY TO SIT

Pup learns the same way Pavlov's dogs learned. Take, for example, sitting. The signal or stimulus is the command "sit." The response is sitting; the reward can be praise or food. The key is to teach the sequence in reverse of what traditional dog training preaches. You must first produce the response, then reward it, so that the response will occur more frequently. When the response is occurring predictably, add the signal prior to the response. After a number of repetitions over a period of time, the signal itself will become effective enough to produce the response.

Sitting, however, is a little more difficult to produce than the salivation in Pavlov's demonstration. Salivating is automatically caused by food. The trainer must take a little more active role to produce the sit response so that it can be followed with a reward. Thus the first part of this training sequence is to produce the response of sitting.

You can usually get a young puppy to sit with food. Puppies tend to be ravenously hungry all the time, so food is a good reward that can be used to shape responses. Every time you feed Pup, go through this sequence:

1. Put his food in a bowl.
2. Put the food under his nose so that he gets a good sniff and knows what it is.
3. Raise the bowl above his head.
4. Wait till he sits.
5. After he sits, immediately put down the bowl for him to eat.
6. While he's eating, praise him with "good dog, good dog."

Of course, the reward is eating. The praise is paired with the act of eating the food, so that praise becomes a reward in itself, for future use. Praise is a lot easier to carry than food, and you always have it with you.

Note that, except for the praise, this process should be carried out in silence. Note also that we have not introduced the signal "sit." Right now we are building the back part of the sequence: response followed by reward. We want food to produce sitting just as in Pavlov's sequence food produced salivation.

The key here is waiting until the desired response occurs before giving the reward by putting down the food bowl. Pup may dance around. He may yap in frustration. He will likely rear up on your leg and scratch. Don't reward any of those behaviors. Do not pair the signal "sit" with any of these behaviors. If you wait long enough, it is inevitable that Pup will sit and look up. Keep your mouth shut and wait. When he does sit, give him the food and verbal praise.

The "sit" sequence: Raise the food bowl over Pup's head, wait till he sits, then put the bowl down so he can eat. Pet and praise him for a job well done.

After several days, the sight of the food bowl above his head at mealtime will cause Pup to sit. Then you add the verbal signal "sit" prior to the response of sitting. After a few of repetitions Pup will sit merely on the signal "sit."

Later you will probably notice, when it is close to mealtime and you are in the area of the house where Pup eats, that he will sit to see if it produces food even when you don't have the food bowl handy.

Note the things you shouldn't do:

1. Don't leave a bowl of food always present. If Pup always has food available and is seldom hungry, then food has little reward value. Keep that in mind when you start feeling guilty about Pup being a little hungry.

   I recommend feeding puppies twice a day on a regular schedule. This makes them easier to house train, since their defecation schedule becomes predictable. Making food available only twice a day also allows them to be trained with food reward. If they are not hungry, food is not a reward.

   Don't let guilt overcome common sense on the feeding schedule. Pup is geared through evolution to eat at well-spaced intervals. In the wolf pack from which he evolved, the mother did not hunt and feed her pups three times a day.

2. Don't cave in while Pup is rearing up and scratching your calves, looking pitifully at you with those big eyes. If you give him the food at that moment, you are not only training him to jump up on you—you are also training him to manipulate you. Wait till he sits to give him the food. It may take five minutes, but it will happen.

TRAINING A YOUNG PUPPY TO STAY

After Pup is consistently sitting on command before getting his food, you can gradually shape that behavior into staying until released to eat.

1. Have Pup sit while keeping the bowl of food above his reach.
2. Put your hand on his chest to physically restrain Pup as you slowly lower the bowl to the floor.
3. Say "sit" one time.
4. After he relaxes and accepts the restraint of your hand, wait a couple of seconds with your hand remaining on his chest, restraining him.
5. Then release him to eat. Use a slight hand motion and a verbal signal such as "OK" to release him.

The "stay" sequence: With Pup sitting, restrain him while you lower the bowl to the floor. Say "stay" and hold him for a few seconds before releasing him to eat with a verbal "OK."

6. After several repetitions of this, try it without the physical restraint. If Pup attempts to charge ahead for the food, simply raise the bowl above his reach. Put him back in place and try it again. Keep repeating until he will sit without restraint, till he is released with a verbal and visual signal.
7. Gradually increase the distance between Pup and the food bowl, and gradually increase the time Pup sits.
8. If your communication skills are not up to the job and you can't get Pup to stay with a restraining hand, then resort to a check cord. Tie a twenty-foot check cord to Pup's collar. Run one end through an anchored object—such as chair leg—behind Pup. Tell Pup to sit, and hold some tension on the cord as you proceed a step or two away and put down the food bowl. Let Pup sit a couple of minutes and then release him with a verbal OK and a hand signal. Gradually stretch out the drill in both time and distance. After a number of repetitions, the behavior will become established and you can eliminate the check cord

Going through this drill with a young puppy is one of the most valuable activities you can engage in. It teaches Pup how to learn through reward, and establishes the foundation for sitting and staying that will make him a calmer, steadier hunting companion in the future.

WHAT'S THE STIMULUS?
When training Pup, you must be aware of what is and what is not a stimulus. Sometimes the stimulus is not what you think. When I was training dogs and running the field-trial circuit, I traveled with sixteen dogs in a dog truck that had individual

traveling compartments. Dogs got out five or six times a day for work and exercise. I would put them back one at a time with a fixed sequence of behavior.

I would call an individual dog over, have him sit, open the door, and tell him "kennel" while giving a slight hand signal. I would stand at the right side of the entrance. The dog would then jump into his compartment. In this sequence the compartment was the reward, because it was his "cave."

After a couple of weeks on the road, the dogs got almost automatic about loading into the truck. One day I tried to put a dog into the truck when I was standing to the left side of his compartment. He wouldn't jump in. After several exaggerated signals, the dog became very agitated and finally ran around behind me and then jumped into the compartment. He had to put me on the right side of the entrance. I learned that standing on the right side of the entrance was part of the signal that he had been conditioned to expect. He had been conditioned through repetition to need all three elements of the signal in order to respond.

A similar thing can happen to the novice trainer. The trainer has the dog sit and stay. Then he walks ten paces away, stops, turns, waits five seconds, and calls the dog with the command "here."

If the trainer does it the same way every time, the dog will usually cue on the other constants in addition to the verbal "here." After a number of repetitions the dog comes automatically, five seconds after the trainer stops and turns. He doesn't wait for the command. The dog is responding to the trainer's behavior sequence in addition to the verbal command. Again, dogs are more prone to learn visual cues than audible ones.

The lesson here is to vary everything except the signal and the response. Change distances, timing, location, etc., so that none accidentally becomes the signal.

Even something as simple as where you're standing when you give a command or signal can become part of that signal if you repeat it enough. The key to training is to vary everything but the signal and response. In this case, change where you're standing now and then when you call the dogs to kennel.

Another frequently seen variation of this phenomenon is the dog that is rigorously trained on obedience in the back yard. He performs perfectly there, but when he is taken elsewhere the obedience disappears. The specific location has become an essential part of the signal. When you take him to a new place, part of the signal is missing. If you follow the same behaviors and patterns and locations all the time, these can become part of the stimulus. If this happens, Pup won't respond without all of the elements present. The solution is to ensure that only the stimulus and response remain consistently the same. Change everything else. Change locations, timing, distractions, and anything else that could become a habit. This requires a little mental effort because, like dogs, we tend to be creatures of habit.

WHAT'S THE REWARD?

The major rewards for Pup, in order of importance, are:

1. **Retrieving.** This is the ultimate reward. A good retriever will leave a bowl of food any time to retrieve something. As we discussed earlier, this retrieving need is a deeply imbedded instinct that Pup inherited through many generations of selective breeding. It is Pup's most powerful motivator, and your secret weapon for training if you use it properly. All you have to do is set things up so that the behaviors preceding any retrieve are the behaviors you want in your dog.

    Of course, as with any reward, too much of a good thing may destroy its attraction. If you give Pup unlimited retrieves every day, you will dilute the value of retrieving as a reward. Also, the retrieving will be the reward for any random behaviors that occur prior to each retrieve. You could thus be building in some behavior problems that will later require punishment to correct.

    Remember that retrieving is an instinct and was inherited by Pup. Retrieving therefore doesn't need a lot of training. The control behaviors are what need training, and retrieving should be the major reward to develop and shape those behaviors.

2. **Petting and Praise.** These are great motivators, but their value can be diluted by overuse. If Pup gets petted and praised all the time, regardless of what he is doing, then petting and praise lose a great deal of their value as rewards for shaping particular behaviors.

    One of the main reasons for raising Pup in the house is to magnify the value of petting and praise as a training tool.

The puppy that is raised inside with the family forms a close bond with family members. They become his pack, and petting and praise from them become much more important to him.

Additionally, praise by itself becomes a much more effective training tool for the dog that has been raised in the house. He will learn to associate praise with the petting that usually accompanies it. Thus the human voice will, by association, become a more valuable motivator for that dog.

A word of caution: There is a universal human tendency to overdo petting and praise. Remember that the goal of training is to produce a calm, well-mannered dog, so don't jack up Pup's emotional state by overrewarding him in the petting and praise department. Usually, a few gentle, calm downward strokes on the top of Pup's shoulders, accompanied by the mild praise "good dog, good dog," are most effective.

3. **Food.** As I mentioned earlier, food is usually an effective reward for young puppies, which grow fast and are usually hungry all the time. In an older dog, however, food becomes less effective. The older dog is usually not a voracious eater, and often has a bowl of food sitting around for him to sample at will. Moreover, your family members may make a hobby out of seeing how much they can feed Pup. When Pup is getting all this food for doing nothing at all, food rewards in training won't have the same allure.

As a demonstration of the relative importance of food as a reward, try a little experiment. While your dog is eating, stand on the other side of the room and praise him. I'll bet he leaves the food and comes over to you. The next time Pup is deeply engaged in a bowl of food, stand across the room and bounce a tennis ball a couple of times. I know he'll leave the food for that. Performing these two experiments will tell you exactly where food ranks in the hierarchy of rewards.

CHAPTER 10

MORE LEARNING

MANY OF THE RESPONSES you need to train are produced by giving Pup an irritating or uncomfortable stimulus that he wants to escape, and by providing the appropriate escape route. Then that response is rewarded in Pavlovian fashion. Here are some examples:

1. **Heeling**. To train Pup to heel you use a choke collar or pinch collar to produce discomfort whenever Pup is away from the "heel zone"—within a foot of your left knee. The escape path is the immediate removal of the neck discomfort when Pup enters the heel zone. Upon entering the heel zone, Pup is rewarded with the verbal praise "good dog, good dog."

2. **Sitting**. How about training an older dog to sit? Our previous discussion concerned a young puppy six weeks to six months old. For an older dog or one that is not so interested in food, we can use an escape response to produce the desired behavior of sitting. This is more akin to the method used by most obedience trainers, with two subtle

(Top) Use a choke or pinch collar to produce discomfort whenever Pup is out of the heel zone. (Bottom) To get Pup to sit, pull straight up, slowly and gently, on the leash, exerting just enough pressure to make him uncomfortable.

differences: (a) The discomfort will be very, very mild, and (b) the timing on your part will be very, very slow.

To begin, put a rope choke collar with leash on Pup. Then, with him standing at your side, pull gently, straight up on the leash. You want to exert just enough pressure so that Pup is uncomfortable. Say nothing. Be quiet. Do not try to rush it.

The object is to produce a response, and that is all. You are not trying to make the response fast or emphatic or anything else. You are merely producing the response of sitting. With the mild discomfort produced by the pressure on his neck, Pup will start fidgeting. That is fine. Keep the same light pressure, because he will soon try to raise his neck higher, which requires lowering his rear and sitting. As soon as he sits, praise and stroke him on the shoulders.

After a few repetitions, Pup will be sitting automatically when he feels a little pressure on the neck. Then you add the signal "sit."

SHAPING THE EMOTIONAL STATE WITHOUT PROZAC

Pavlovian conditioning also applies to emotional states. You can modify Pup's emotional response with training. In the traditional retriever-training regimen, Pavlovian conditioning works against developing a steady dog by rewarding the emotional state of being wired up. The bird falls, causing Pup to get extremely excited, and while he's sitting there bouncing on his toes on the edge of breaking, we send him on the retrieve within a few seconds of the fall. We just rewarded Pup for being on the edge of disobedience. It's not a very long step for him to go over that edge.

We should be using Pavlovian conditioning to make Pup calmer and steadier. It is simply a matter of changing the timing. To train Pup to be calm, simply wait until he's calmed down before sending him on the retrieve. After the bird or dummy falls, wait five or ten minutes, whatever it takes, until Pup becomes calm and relaxes a little. Then send him on the retrieve. You are thus rewarding the proper emotional state of calmness. That's how you get a calm but hard-working dog.

The retriever world tends to confuse the calm dog with the dog that lacks retrieving desire. This is generally not the case. A properly trained dog can be calm when he needs to be, and hard-going when it comes time to retrieve the birds.

The widely held perception of a calm dog lacking retrieving desire is more likely related to widespread faulty training practices. A typical dog is thrown several thousand dummies as he is growing up. He will not be restrained in any fashion on any of these retrieves. Thus he is trained to break and retrieve at will.

Then, when the dog is eighteen or twenty months old, we change the rules and start requiring him to be steady. This usually requires a considerable degree of punishment to steady him. The dog, used to a long history of breaking, is as likely to associate the punishment with retrieving. Thus he sometimes slows down or quits retrieving. The fault certainly doesn't lie with the dog. He is not low on retrieving desire. He's simply had his retrieving desire punished excessively.

Hanging in There When the Going Gets Tough
How about Pup hunting up birds that fall into heavy cover? How do you produce a dog that has initiative and perseverance in tough conditions? You don't do it by making every training session a final exam. You do this by gradually building up the level of difficulty while keeping each individual training session simple enough that Pup is always successful. You make sure that Pup

finds the bird while he's hunting with enthusiasm and confidence. This is another case, like steadiness, where you are training not only a behavior sequence, but an emotional state as well.

There are several practices that will help ensure Pup's success on work that becomes increasingly difficult in both distance and depth of cover. On long retrieves, especially those in heavy cover, start short. Have someone throw out the dummies, and start with Pup only 30 to 40 yards from the thrower. Then back up for subsequent retrieves, with the thrower throwing the bird in roughly the same area each time. By backing up in 25-yard increments you can have Pup confidently retrieving a bird falling 200 yards out.

If conditions are such that you can't back up, such as in a water retrieve, throw an insurance bird while Pup is on the way to a mark or blind. If you are working Pup on a 100-yard retrieve, and are not positive that he will be successful, add some insurance. When Pup is 50 yards out, on the way to retrieve the bird that has just been thrown by your helper, have your helper throw another bird into the same area as the first.

Another practice to ensure success, especially in heavy cover, is "salting the area." Toss six or eight birds within a 50-foot circle. Your helper then throws a bird into this area while you work the dog from some distance away. The extra birds lying around the area of the fall ensure quick success for Pup on a difficult exercise.

TESTING IS NO SUBSTITUTE FOR TRAINING
Don't fall into the common trap of going out every day and setting up a new "test" to see if Pup can do it. That's a sure way of training Pup to fail.

Sometimes a trainer will switch from dummies to birds in an attempt to increase an unmotivated dog's interest in retrieving. He's trying to compensate for poor training by increasing the magnitude of the reward. It does not work. If you test instead of train, you still end up with a dog that has low motivation levels.

EXTINCTION OF BEHAVIOR: WHY PUP STOPS DOING SOMETHING

Just because you train a behavior into Pup doesn't mean it will always be there. There are two basic things that may cause Pup to cease performing a certain behavior. He may cease performing because you've lost your pack leader status, or he may cease performing because the reward has gone away.

DOMINANCE INFLUENCES RESPONSIVENESS

Looking first at the dominance factor, you can say that Pup will cease performing some behaviors consistently when you lose your dominant position with him. You've no doubt seen instances of this. Frequently, a dog that is quite responsive to its owner will be much less responsive to other family members. That dog will perform well for the owner but doesn't obey the owner's wife or children. My current gun dog is a sterling example of this. Jake minds me impeccably. He obeys my wife when he feels like it. This is a case of a lack of dominance causing a lack of response.

CLASSIC EXTINCTION THEORY

From the Pavlovian conditioning viewpoint, a behavior becomes extinct over time when the reward is withheld. This can occur fairly quickly or over a longer period. The difference comes from the schedule of reinforcement used during the conditioning process. There are two choices, a constant schedule of reinforcement and a variable schedule of reinforcement.

For a constant schedule of reinforcement, you reward the dog every time he performs the behavior. For instance, if you are training him to sit, you pet him every time he sits. A behavior conditioned on a constant schedule of reinforcement is not very resistant to extinction.

The human parallel for a constant schedule of reinforcement would be a slot machine that paid off every time you cranked the handle. Suddenly the slot machine stops paying after consistently paying for a hundred cranks. You would soon quit pulling the handle in the absence of reward. Likewise, the dog that has been trained to sit on a constant schedule of reinforcement will not retain that response very long if the reward is terminated.

Contrast the constant schedule of reinforcement to a variable schedule of reinforcement, where a behavior is rewarded in an infrequent and unpredictable manner. Again the human counterpoint is the slot machine. Slot machines are in actuality programmed to pay off infrequently and in an unpredictable manner. Walk into any casino and you can see the evidence of the longevity of the behavior learned on a variable schedule of reinforcement.

Schedules of reinforcement can work for you or against you. As the owner of a new puppy, you might expect the following scenario when first confining the puppy to a dog crate as part of house training:

1. You put the puppy in the crate in the kitchen so you can take him outside quickly when he exits the crate.
2. You go to bed.
3. The puppy whines and cries, and after five minutes you go and stand in front of the crate and say, "Hush! Hush!"
4. The puppy hushes and you go back to bed.
5. The puppy whines and cries again. This time you wait seven minutes and then go stand in front of the crate and say, "Hush! Hush!"
6. The puppy hushes and you go back to bed.
7. The puppy whines and cries again. This time you only wait three minutes to go to the crate.
8. After two weeks you wonder why your puppy is so stupid that he cannot learn to be quiet.

What is really happening here is that the "Hush! Hush!" that you think is a punishment is really a reward to Pup in the form of attention. Thus you are actually rewarding the undesirable crying behavior. Moreover, the reward (attention) is being given on a variable schedule, so you are actually making it harder for Pup to stop the behavior.

You can also use the persistence of a variable schedule of reinforcement to work for you. One of your main goals should be to produce a steady, calm dog. The dog is started on a constant schedule of reinforcement, but is quickly changed to a variable schedule. A variable schedule of reinforcement greatly strengthens that calmness and steadiness.

As soon as the steadiness behavior is somewhat established, you should pick up a lot of the retrieves yourself or with another dog in an unpredictable pattern. Pup should be allowed to retrieve only about 25 percent of the dummies or birds that he sees fall in training. However, don't get in the habit of giving Pup every fourth retrieve or any other fixed pattern. Mix it up so that the reinforcement is random and unpredictable. Then you have a variable schedule of reinforcement for steadiness, and the steadiness will be much more resistant to extinction.

CHAPTER 11

ELIMINATING
BAD BEHAVIOR

PUNISHMENT

Punishment is used to eliminate undesirable behavior more quickly than simply withholding a reward. The easiest way to avoid using punishment in the training process is to keep Pup from developing undesirable behaviors. Identify bad behavior and change it quickly before it becomes firmly entrenched.

Unfortunately, few of us are perfect trainers. Thus we occasionally have to use some form of punishment in the training process.

There is a distinct window of time during which punishment is effective. Punishment works to discourage behavior that immediately precedes it. Be careful that you are punishing the behavior you want to eliminate.

Take, for example, the case of breaking. Pup breaks and you punish him by giving him a good shake. The obvious criticism here is that the situation should have been engineered so that Pup was not tempted to break in the first place...you should have been out in front, the throw should have been shorter and lower.

If breaking does occur, the next best thing is to punish it at the right time in the behavior sequence. Therefore we will assume that you have a check cord on Pup and that your foot is on the check cord. Then when he breaks, you can immediately get him and shake him as punishment. The breaking would thus be nipped in the bud.

Keeping a check cord on Pup during training helps you control him and punish him at the right time in the behavior sequence.

What if you don't have a check cord on Pup? He breaks and succeeds in getting the retrieve. Then you can forget the punishment. Otherwise the punishment will simply help extinguish the behaviors of coming and retrieving.

Another classic example: Pup runs away. You run after him. You finally get within thirty feet of him, call him to you, and punish him. Punishing Pup after you have called him to you is extinguishing the behavior of coming when called. Obviously, this is another no-win situation.

Both of these examples emphasize the value of the check cord in dog training. This is especially true for the trainer who might be going a little too fast, who might be asking too much of the dog or testing instead of training. Those are generally the conditions that produce situations requiring punishment. Without the check cord you have no ability to use punishment at the right time in the behavior sequence.

In addition to eliminating unwanted behaviors, punishment can also be used to make some places off-limits. Pup doesn't like to go back to a place where he's had an unpleasant experience. If you don't want him exploring the kitchen counter, put a couple of mousetraps up there and let one bite him. He probably won't return. The same process can be used to keep Pup off your furniture and out of the flowerbeds.

Of course, an alternative is to have Pup roaming loose only when you are handy and alert to supervise him. Then you can teach him to stay off counters, furniture, etc. When he's not supervised he should be in his crate. Again, if you don't let Pup get started in undesirable behavior, he doesn't develop bad habits.

WHAT'S THE PUNISHMENT?

To determine how to use punishment, we have merely to look once again at pack behavior in wolves. Those same ancestral behaviors work in dogs. As we saw in chapter 5, there are basically four mechanisms used in the pack to enforce dominance and hence discipline. In order of increasing severity, these are:

1. The pack leader delivers a direct, threatening stare.
2. The pack leader looms over the subordinate by standing tall and raising his hackles.
3. The pack leader lays his head over the shoulder of a subordinate or rears up and puts his paws on the subordinate's shoulders.
4. The pack leader charges the subordinate, rolls it on its back, seizes it by the throat, and shakes it vigorously while growling fiercely.

These are very effective punishments to use on your dog. Obviously, you gear the severity to the nature of the individual dog.

Use canine mechanisms for punishment. For serious infractions, grab Pup by the scruff of the neck and hindquarters and shake him, lifting all four of his feet off the ground.

THE STARTLE RESPONSE

The startle response occurs when you reach out and touch Pup at some distance. The distance can be 5 feet, or it can be 500 feet. Ideally, you invoke it at 15 to 20 feet and never let Pup learn that there is any limit on distance.

Take Pup out for an off-leash walk, and wait until he is thoroughly engrossed in sniffing a bush 15 to 20 feet away from you. He should be looking away from you, so that he receives no visual signal. Take the leash from your pocket, wad it up, and throw it at Pup. As it hits him, say "here." Pup will jump like a startled rabbit and scoot to you quickly. The occasional use of this tactic will keep Pup a lot more manageable when he is off the leash.

ELECTRIC COLLARS

As I mentioned in chapter 3, if you can't train a dog without the electric collar, you probably can't train him with it. If you have not done the homework to become a good dog trainer, the electric collar will probably do more harm than good. For the knowledgeable, skillful, professional dog trainer, the electric collar is a very effective and useful training tool. For the novice trainer, who has not spent the time to develop the necessary training skills, the electric collar is frequently a disaster.

To develop the training skills necessary to use the electric collar properly, the novice trainer would have to read a couple of books on the subject, and then spend at least a couple of weeks working with and watching a good professional trainer. Even then, the dog must first be trained by conventional methods. After the dog is well grounded in obedience, that obedience is reinforced by a thorough conditioning program with the electric collar in controlled situations. However, since most hunters and dog owners are not going to take the time or trouble to use the electric collar properly, they should not use it at all.

The other essential element for successful use of the electric collar is a calm, objective trainer. It is very easy for a professional trainer to be calm and objective. He is training twenty or more dogs a day. He has learned through experience that allowing anger and frustration to cloud his judgment merely sends the training program backwards. He has schooled himself in objectivity, and he doesn't have a large emotional investment in those twenty dogs.

The typical hunter, however, has one dog, and he wants that dog to do everything well. The one-dog person tends to become more easily frustrated and angry when training is not going the way he expects. The electric collar is far too easy to use. It requires merely the touch of a button. The one-dog person is much more prone to use the electric collar inappropriately, on a dog that doesn't deserve punishment.

There is also a less obvious but more far-reaching effect of the electric collar. Widespread use of the electric collar will, over time, have an adverse effect on breeding selection. The electric collar enables a good trainer to train marginal dogs that might be very difficult to train by conventional methods. Dogs that might have high pain thresholds, or that might be hyperactive or unusually dominant. Whatever the cause of the dog's uncooperative nature, a good trainer can probably train him with an electric collar. The trainer might assume that any behavior problems the dog had early in life will not be inherited by his puppies. Unfortunately, that dog's personality disorder will probably be inherited by a percentage of his puppies.

As more and more trainers use the electric collar, more marginal dogs will be capable of being trained to high standards, and we will see an increase in dogs that are less tractable. Again, we should be breeding dogs that are easily trained without electric collars.

USING THE ELECTRIC COLLAR
Although the electric collar has a very bad influence on breeding selection, properly used it is probably the most humane

training tool for training a tough, uncooperative dog. Moreover, the electric collar is probably necessary to compete in today's field trials.

The key to using the electric collar is in the pre-training. The responses that you are going to condition with the electric collar must already be trained into Pup. Then you have a high probability of eliciting the appropriate response when you shock Pup with the collar.

The electric collar operates on the principle of the escape response. Dogs try to escape pain. To be successful you must ensure that the desired response will occur. Pup must be on a check cord for initial collar work so that you can control the responses.

THE MECHANICS OF ELECTRIC COLLAR TRAINING

If you simply take Pup to the field, strap on the collar, and give him a shock, he is going to respond by attempting to escape the shock. He will either run from you or to you as fast as he can. If he runs away, you will find him in a few hours. If he runs to you, you may have trouble getting him to leave your side for a while. Either way, you have not provided the desired escape route.

To train with the electric collar you must:

1. Establish and train the escape responses.
2. Completely control the setting.

Going through the conditioning process establishes the appropriate escape responses and teaches Pup not to be afraid of the electric collar.

Assuming that Pup has already been trained in obedience, the first step to introduce the electric collar is to take Pup back through some basic on-leash obedience drills. Reinforce his coming, sitting, and staying behavior for a session or two in the yard. Use the choke collar or pinch collar to reinforce the responses. For example, to get Pup to sit, say "sit" and pull on the leash to apply pressure to his neck. To get him to come, say "here" and tug on the leash.

After a brief review to ensure that the responses are present and sharp, add the shock of the electric collar. The shock of the collar will replace the pull and tug of the choke collar.

Lesson One:
1. Do four or five "sit" routines with just leash pressure on Pup's neck. Don't forget to praise him after the correct response.

2. Do the next "sit" sequence with leash pressure and a quick shock. Praise Pup after he sits.

3. Try a longer shock that ceases as Pup's rear hits the ground, so that Pup learns to turn off the shock by sitting. Praise him after he sits.

4. Give another "sit" command with shock. Praise him after he sits.

5. With Pup sitting, step out to end of the five-foot leash. Pull gently till Pup's rear comes off the ground. Give the "sit" command with shock to get his rear back on the ground. Praise him after he sits. (It is very important to establish the escape response when Pup is out away from you. Otherwise, any time you shock Pup in the field his response will probably be to come to you.)

6. Pull gently again, while standing five feet away. Pull with gradually increasing strength until Pup's butt again comes off the ground. Command "sit" and give a shock to get his rear back on the ground. Walk over and pet and praise him after he sits.

7. Attach a thirty-foot check cord to Pup's collar. Sit Pup with a slight shock, and then step fifteen feet away. Pull steadily on Pup's neck till his butt is off the ground. Command "sit" and give a shock to get his butt back on ground. Walk over and pet and praise him after he is sitting.

8. Sit Pup and walk out to the end of the thirty-foot check cord. Jerk Pup toward you while commanding "here."

Note that, in keeping with the principle of never training-in a behavior that must later be extinguished, we reinforced all three behaviors in the first session. It is, however, critical to reinforce sitting first.

Also, use a variable-intensity collar, trying the lightest setting first and increasing it if Pup does not respond.

CHAPTER **12**

RAISING PUP
IN THE HOUSE

IF I HAD TO RECOMMEND one thing to make retriever training easier, it would be to raise Pup in the house with your family. Raising Pup in the house accomplishes two major goals:

1. It establishes your family as Pup's "pack." This pack bonding is the source of Pup's responsiveness to the pack leader, which we typically describe as "desire to please." Additionally, the pack structure elicits in Pup the need to read the behavior and signals of pack members. Pup starts focusing attention on humans.

2. It forces you and your family to spend time with Pup, and vice versa. Thus clear lines of communication are established. Much of this communication is on a subconscious level, in the form of body language, motion, and posture. This nonverbal communication is Pup's natural language.

HOUSEBREAKING
Raising Pup in the house is easy. Most people perceive housebreaking as the biggest obstacle. It is not. Retrievers are clean

by nature. Unless you force them to, they will not soil their own nests.

Unfortunately, many breeders inadvertently train puppies to mess in their own nests by confining them too long to the whelping box. When a bitch has a litter of puppies, she cleans them and ingests their bodily wastes until they begin eating solid food at about four or five weeks old.

By this age the puppies are sufficiently coordinated to walk, and they will waddle out of the "nest" to defecate. If there is no exit, they can't leave and are thus inadvertently trained to soil their nests.

A pup that has not been "trained" to soil the house will be much easier to housebreak. Even the pup that starts with a handicap is quite trainable. The key is to use Pup's natural inclination to keep his nest clean.

REINFORCE THE GOOD HABIT

Housebreaking is not accomplished through punishment. The key is to never let Pup get started in urinating or defecating in the house. Then you don't have undesirable behavior to try to eliminate. All you have to do is know when Pup is likely to need to relieve himself. Then you can take him outdoors before it happens. The predictability is achieved with a dog crate and with scheduling.

THE MAGIC CRATE

Get Pup a dog crate. A crate that is too large will allow him to soil one end and sleep at the other end, so get one that is just large enough for him to turn around and lie down in. Again, Pup will naturally go to great lengths to avoid soiling his nest. To help him achieve this goal, you must take him directly outside every time he is taken from the crate.

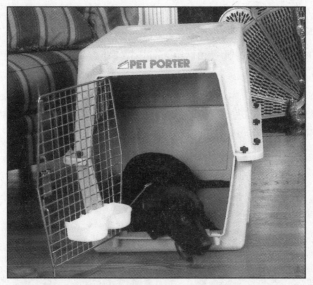

Contrary to popular opinion, a dog really is at home in the close confines of his "cave"—er, crate.

THE SCHEDULE

A regular schedule is important in housebreaking. Pup should be taken outside at regular intervals. A good schedule is one that conforms to yours, such as:

1. When you get up in the morning.
2. After breakfast.
3. After lunch.
4. After dinner.
5. Just before you go to bed.

Again, these outdoor excursions should occur at the same time every day, regardless of Pup's activities. Take him out every day at the same time after lunch, whether he's been in the crate for three hours or just fifteen minutes. Pup cannot speak English; therefore, he can only predict the schedule by what has happened in the past.

Also of great importance is Pup's feeding schedule. He should be fed at the same times every day. This will tend to make him defecate at the same times every day. Take him out immediately after he has eaten or had a drink of water. Additionally, it is often helpful to reduce the amount and num-

Walks in the city should be on leash, and should include a variety of environments to help the dogs learn to function in different surroundings.

ber of times he's fed during the housebreaking period. Feeding him twice a day will probably work best.

It will be easy for Pup to make it through the night if he is given no food or water after 5:00 in the evening. Then, if he is taken outdoors at 9:00 p.m. or 10:00 p.m., he should be able to make it through the night.

CHEWING ON FURNITURE AND FIXTURES

Most Puppies like to chew on things. To preserve your furniture, and marriage, you should direct that chewing into socially acceptable channels. First, keep Pup in his crate when he is not supervised. Then give him some acceptable chewing objects such as rawhide chew toys, etc. Pet stores sell a huge variety of these items.

Next, teach him not to chew on everything else. When he is under supervision and starts chewing on furniture, walk over and give him a sharp finger thump on the snout, followed by a verbal "no." When he's not under supervision, he should be confined to his crate.

If Pup has very strong tendencies to chew and you find yourself having to thump him more than once or twice, you need to attach a five- or six-foot length of cord to his collar and let him trail it when he is loose in the house. When he begins chewing on something, get your foot on the cord before you thump him on the snout. Otherwise you will find yourself training Pup to run away from you.

MAJOR BENEFICIAL ACTIVITIES FOR PUPPIES

During Pup's first six months, he does not need a lot of regimented training. He needs to be a puppy. One of the most important things you can do during this stage is to train him to act civilized in the house. Another is to take him for walks in both the city and the country.

In addition to the aforementioned housebreaking and no-chew training, you should train Pup to sit for his supper as described in chapter 9. Additional activities might include having Pup at your feet while you are watching television or reading the paper. Tie a short length of cord to his collar. When you are reading or watching television, put your foot on the cord. Pup will learn to lie quietly at your feet.

To train Pup on steadiness while you're reading a paper or watching TV, attach a cord to his collar and put your foot on the other end of the cord.

Walks in the city should be on a leash to protect Pup from traffic, and these walks should include a variety of environments such as shopping centers, busy traffic, etc. This will help

Pup become skillful and comfortable in dealing with new and confusing environments.

Walks in the country are very valuable to Pup. Take him off the leash. He learns all sorts of new sights and sounds when you take him for a long walk in the woods and fields. He learns to stay with you, and if you'll pet him whenever he comes up, he learns to like being around you. These unfettered country walks help develop his hunting instincts, get him started in using that wonderful nose.

Another major benefit of walks in the country is the development of Pup's agility skills. If you take him over gradually tougher terrain with ditches, steep hillsides, rocks, and crevices, he will develop the agility of a mountain goat in a surprisingly short time.

When I was training search-and-rescue teams, the handlers would spend hours harassing their dogs to get them to climb ladders and walk planks. I found that a retriever who had a good foundation of rough-terrain walks would do the agility tests with ease.

Again, the one activity that puppies do not need much of is retrieving. Retrieving is an instinctive behavior they are born with. A lot of uncontrolled retrieving with young puppies simply establishes undesirable breaking behavior that must be extinguished later. Two or three retrieves a week are plenty for a puppy younger than six months.

COMMENTS ON DOG CRATES

One invariably encounters criticisms of the use of dog crates to confine a dog. To answer those criticisms I offer a couple of observations gleaned from training and knowing thousands of dogs over the past thirty years. A crate is a very natural place to a puppy. In the wild, wolves normally whelp in a den dug into the ground. Thus the dog crate becomes Pup's cave or den.

Additionally, years of observing dog behavior have led me to the following conclusion. When you leave a dog in a five-acre pen, or when you leave a dog in a dog crate and walk away, the dog's reaction is the same. He curls up behind the gate and goes to sleep, awaiting your return.

You will find that Pup, after a week or so of living in the crate, will start going in on his own when he's tired of playing. If you leave the crate door open, you will probably discover that the crate is Pup's preferred sleeping spot.

CHAPTER 13

OBEDIENCE AS A
WAY OF LIFE

NOT A FIFTEEN-MINUTE DRILL

The good news is that an obedient dog is a real pleasure to live with. The bad news is that obedience takes some degree of commitment from you, Pup's pack leader. For Pup, obedience is a way of life. It is not something that a daily fifteen-minute training session will magically impart.

A key to obedience training is for you to maintain your position as pack leader. This is done through requiring obedience all the time, not just during training sessions. You can spend two hours a day doing obedience training sessions, but if you let Pup disobey during the other twenty-two hours, you will not have an obedient dog. Require him to obey all the time and he will be very responsive.

Obedience training is easy. You can train Pup to heel, sit, and stay in five or six lessons. The tough part is requiring him to respond the rest of the time. Just because you've taught him to heel, sit, and stay doesn't mean he is going to automatically do it from now on. Quite the contrary: Pup is going to regularly challenge the limits you place on him. The frequency of the challenges will be directly proportional to your consistency. If you are very consistent, Pup will rarely disobey. If you squelch the small rebellions, then the big ones never occur. Pup understands the program and is happy.

OBEDIENCE IS NOT FOR EVERYONE

Again, just because Pup obeys you doesn't mean he's going to obey anyone else. He will obey only those whom he perceives to be dominant in the pack hierarchy. He can obey you perfectly, but he will not obey your wife unless she maintains her dominance by requiring consistent responses from him.

A good measure of Pup's relative dominance is whether he can put his paws on you. Again, one of the behaviors that the pack leader uses to reinforce dominance is to rear up and put his front paws on the shoulders of a subordinate. The subordinate

If a dog respects your dominance, he will be psychologically incapable of jumping up and putting his paws on you.

is psychologically incapable of putting his front paws on a dominant pack member.

I used to regularly demonstrate this at the first session of my obedience courses. I would take a dog from one of the students and entice him to put his front paws on me. It was usually very easy to get him to jump up on me.

After putting him through a short obedience lesson, I would try again to get him to jump on me. Invariably, the dog would be unable to put his paws on me because the obedience established my dominance. Frequently, prolonged enticement from me would get the pup razzed up enough that he just had to jump on someone. Though I was the one enticing him to jump on me, he would run over and jump on his owner, ten feet away. This was a great illustration of the power of obedience in reinforcing dominance, and of the mechanism of rearing up on a subordinate.

OBEDIENCE DEFINED

Obedience consists of three simple behaviors: heeling, sitting, and coming. Pup is heeling when he is walking along at your side with his nose within a foot or so of your knee. Heeling is typically on the left side for the right-handed shooter to keep the dog out of the way of the gun. If you are left-handed, reverse it, or if you want to make Pup ambidextrous, have him heel on either side.

Coming, of course, means coming when called.

Sitting is a two-for-one command. Pup should sit on command, and should also stay where he's sitting until told to do otherwise. Thus "sit" also means "stay."

These basic behaviors can be taught in about three to five twenty-minute training sessions. The challenge is to ingrain these habits into Pup so that he will consistently respond when he's farther away, or when he's facing extreme distraction and temptation.

THE MYTH OF REFRESHER TRAINING

When I was running Wildrose Kennels and training up to thirty dogs a day, I used to love to see dogs coming back for refresher training. The owner brought the dog back because his responsiveness had gradually deteriorated over the intervening year. These dogs were absolute gravy. A couple of obedience training sessions would snap a dog back into his former responsiveness, and he would become a real pleasure to work for the next month or two. All of his training was still there—he just needed a pack leader to bring it out.

The secret is in knowing the trigger for responsiveness. Dogs don't "forget" behaviors that have been trained. They may become unresponsive, but they don't forget. All you have to do is reestablish your position as the pack leader, and his responsiveness will return. The simplest, most gentle way to do this is through obedience training and obedience drills.

Obedience is the foundation of all subsequent trained behaviors, as well as the foundation for responsiveness. Train Pup well in obedience, and keep requiring responsiveness, and you can get him to do anything. Even better, you can get him to do anything without the heavy use of force.

THE WRONG WAY

To illustrate how to start obedience training, let me first explain the wrong way to train. Unfortunately, this wrong method is all too prevalent in the dog-training community at large. It involves a choke collar and a lot of dragging and nagging, while the handler shouts commands that have absolutely no meaning to Pup. Here is how it goes:

Put a choke collar on Pup and start dragging him along, holding him at your left knee, all the while barking "Heel! Heel!" Do this daily for two weeks and Pup will learn to heel in spite of the training program. After you've got Pup well programmed to heel and keep himself right beside you, start trying to get Pup to stay while you move away from him.

Let me tell you what is really happening here. When you put that choke collar on Pup and start dragging him along, you are triggering an opposing response in Pup that makes him pull harder against the choke collar. He's being choked and his neck feels uncomfortable when he's in the very location that you are trying to teach him to seek. When he's by your left knee, his neck hurts. The hurting neck makes him want to leave that space by your left knee. Meanwhile, you're yelling, "Heel! Heel! Heel!"

In such circumstances, guess what "Heel!" means to Pup. From Pup's perspective, it means, "My neck is hurting and I want to leave this space by this guy's left knee." What's amazing is that dogs are adaptive and flexible enough to eventually get trained in spite of such methods.

❖

THE RIGHT WAY
LESSON ONE

Your demeanor and attitude are all-important. Pup's primary means of communication is body language and attitude. You better believe that he is a master at reading you. Your attitude should be positive, businesslike, and authoritative. Conduct yourself in a manner that conveys that you expect compliance.

This discussion of obedience is geared toward dogs six months and older. This is the most important training session of Pup's career, because this session is going to greatly influence how he views training in general. Make sure he's successful. Then you can reward him. That way Pup will learn and enjoy himself at the same time. We are going to teach him to heel, sit, stay, and come in this first lesson.

Heeling is the most important part of initial obedience training because, when done properly, it teaches Pup that you are the pack leader. Heeling also trains Pup to watch you, the handler. The dominance of the pack leader elicits the response from Pup.

Again, watching the handler is vital to communicating, since most of Pup's communication is visual. Likewise, it is very difficult for Pup to respond to a voice command in the absence of some visual signal. So to make training easy, we need to teach Pup to watch the handler early on.

The first step is make sure Pup has learned to give to neck. If he's ever been tied to an immovable object, then he's probably learned to give to his neck. If he's been dragged around on a leash, he's also probably learned. The test is to tie him to a tree and walk away. Use a non-slip collar. If he doesn't fight the restraint, then he has obviously already learned to give to neck. If he does fight the restraint, keep some distance from him and let him keep fighting the restraint till he gives in to it. You would rather Pup had this particular argument with a tree than with his trainer. It will make learning to heel much simpler.

Be careful not to let Pup overheat in very hot weather. If he gets frantic about it, calm him with reassuring vocalizations. When he quits fighting the restraint, he's learned to give to his neck, and you are ready to continue to the next phase, heeling

First, put a choke collar on Pup. (I prefer one made of regular rope to the chain ones. The chain collar doesn't release as quickly and smoothly as rope.) Next attach a six-foot leash to the collar, and start walking. Keep your eyes on Pup. When he's in the heel zone with his nose within a foot or so of your knee, the leash should be slack, and you should be saying, "Good dog, good dog." When he gets ahead of you, extend your arm to give him additional slack, then turn—quickly and quietly— 180 degrees and walk briskly in the opposite direction. Suddenly Pup gets a healthy tug on the neck that spins him around and starts moving him in the other direction. Simultaneously, he looks up and finds that he's six feet behind you and way outside the heel zone. The discomfort occurs outside the heel zone. He hurries to catch up. When he is in the heel zone you say, "Good dog, good dog."

Five important things are happening here:

1. Pup feels the discomfort of the tug on his neck when he's outside the heel zone, the comfort of the slack leash and verbal praise when he's inside the zone.

2. That forceful tug at the end of the leash imparts your opposite momentum to Pup and jerks him around toward you, lifting his front feet off the ground. This forceful shift of his weight is very important. It triggers a subordinate response in Pup. Again, your change of direction should be extreme and crisp and forceful enough to lift Pup's front feet off the ground. Shifting Pup's front feet off the ground signals that you are his pack leader.

3. Pup is getting a reward in the form of verbal praise when he's inside the heel zone.

4. Pup is learning that it's his responsibility to watch you and keep himself at heel. When he's not paying attention, he suddenly finds himself out at the end of the leash with you moving rapidly in the other direction.

5. Pup is not associating any commands with these fragments of behavior, because you are not giving any commands. You will save that for after the behavior is formed. After Pup is heeling properly, you start using the command "heel." Then Pup will associate the command with the appropriate behavior.

Continue this first session in silence except for the praise when Pup is in the heel zone. It is very important to keep your eyes and attention on Pup. Whenever he gets out front, or focuses his attention elsewhere, repeat your about-face. After four or five of these maneuvers, Pup will be looking at you and keeping himself at heel. Then you may start using the command.

Two other behaviors will occur in some dogs: lagging behind and leg hugging. Lagging is overcompensation on Pup's part as he modifies his hard-charging behavior. Pup finds that in front is not the place to be, and thus tries lagging behind you. The solution is to walk faster and give a good tug on Pup as he falls farther behind. As you get him back in the heel zone, praise him some more. He will correct himself very quickly.

Leg hugging is an attempt by Pup to avoid the mental effort of watching you with his eyes to keep himself at heel. Pup will move in close so that he is touching your leg. Then he can tell by sense of touch when you are turning—he doesn't have to focus much attention on you.

To discourage this behavior, simply turn into him. Every time he moves into physical contact with your leg, turn rapidly and forcefully and walk briskly into him. Keep walking into him until he moves away from your leg. One or two repetitions are usually enough to modify Pup's behavior. Then he will use his eyes to keep himself in the proper position, and you will be reinforcing a very important communication habit.

AN EFFECTIVE TRAINING COLLAR

Some degree of hand-eye coordination and motor skill is needed to perform the initial obedience drills. Also required is a degree of timing. I have noticed over ten years of teaching obedience classes that a lot of people have difficulty managing the timing issue with a standard choke collar. Additionally, small people with large dogs sometimes don't have the strength needed to properly modify Pup's behavior during the initial obedience lessons.

The JASA training collar, also known as a pinch collar, is a simple solution. This is a very stiff leather slip-collar with brass tacks protruding on the inside. The tacks are a little too sharp on a new collar and should be dulled slightly with a file.

The pinch collar looks mean but is very effective. In fact, the pinch collar is much kinder to Pup than a handler with poor timing, jerking Pup around inappropriately and thus prolonging his discomfort. The pinch collar eliminates timing and coordination problems and makes the lessons crisp, effective, and brief.

To begin heeling, you simply put the collar on with the roller to the outside, away from you. Then you grasp the leash about eighteen inches from the collar, keep your hand extended down and locked at your left side, and start walking. When Pup forges ahead he makes the collar constrict and pinch his neck.

He will automatically slow to release it. The same occurs when he lags behind. Pup is in control of the collar when you keep your hand immobilized, and he quickly teaches himself to remain in the heel zone. Dogs will not abuse themselves when they are controlling the pinch of this collar.

On the quick turns, much less muscle power is required from the handler due to the leverage given by the pinch collar. A few rapid reverses of direction during heeling drills will have Pup watching you closely and keeping himself in the heel zone.

SITTING AND STAYING

Sitting and staying should be taught in the first obedience lesson. Again, this is in keeping with a basic tenant of dog training: Don't train in a behavior that you have to train out later. Heeling trains Pup to stay right beside you. Training Pup to stay involves you moving away from him. Before you get him thoroughly programmed to stick right beside your left knee, it would be wise to start teaching him that it is also OK to be away from you.

During this first obedience lesson, after Pup has started heeling a little, teach him to sit. As you are walking along with Pup at heel, stop and hold a mild tension upward on the leash. You want just enough pressure make Pup uncomfortable and to make him want to do something to relieve the discomfort. If you are holding light tension straight up, then the natural thing for Pup to do is raise his head by sitting. If you hold a steady pressure as he fidgets, he will decide to sit. As his rear hits the ground, give the command "sit." Then stroke Pup gently on the shoulder and say, "Good dog, good dog." Pup will associate the command with the appropriate response. Do not say "sit" prior

After Pup sits, raise your hand in the traffic cop gesture. Command "sit" and step away from him. If he moves, command "sit" again.

to the action of sitting—otherwise Pup forms the wrong association. You don't want the command "sit" associated with fidgeting behavior.

Repeat this sitting sequence a few times and Pup will be sitting automatically as you stop walking. Now add the "stay" behavior. After Pup sits, raise your hand in a traffic cop's "stop" gesture. Command "sit." Take one step away from Pup while watching him closely. If he starts to move, command "sit" again to keep him there. Let Pup sit a couple of seconds and then step back beside him. Stroke him gently on the shoulder and say, "Good dog, good dog." Keep your voice gentle and calm. Remember, you do not want to overdo the praise and excite Pup. That emotional state is not conducive to obedient behavior.

Repeat this sequence but take two steps away, being careful to keep Pup in place with your arm raised in the traffic cop gesture and your eyes fixed on his in a direct stare. Again, step back to him and calmly praise him while gently stroking his shoulders. Repeat this sequence four or five times, extending the distance between you and Pup each time. By the fourth or fifth repetition you should be out near the end of the leash and three or four steps from Pup.

TRAINING PUP TO COME

We are still in the first lesson and have so far taught Pup to heel, sit, and stay. We want to end the lesson with coming. For training Pup to come to you, the best command is "here." "Here" can be projected with authority to a distant Pup. Thus it is the command of choice.

Begin with Pup sitting. Give the traffic cop gesture, step out to the end of the leash, and pause to let him sit a few seconds. Then give a tug on the leash. As Pup starts coming, give the command "here" in a calm, authoritative voice. Repeat this sequence a couple of times. Finish your lesson by having Pup stay while you move out to the end of the leash. Now walk over to him and stroke him gently on the shoulders a couple of times.

There is a reason for mixing up the pattern by returning to Pup in this second sequence. Whatever you do consistently, Pup will learn to anticipate. If you have him sit, then walk six feet away, turn, wait five seconds, and call him to you—that's the habit he will form. Do it enough and he will become unable to sit longer than the five seconds he has been programmed to sit.

LESSON TWO: REPEAT LESSON ONE

Lesson two is very easy. You simply repeat what you've started in lesson one. Do a little heeling, sitting, staying, and coming. Make Pup stay a little in lesson two. Keep the lesson short and try to conduct it so that Pup is successful on every command. Ten minutes is plenty.

LESSON THREE: REPEAT AGAIN

Change equipment here. Trade your six-foot leash for a twenty-foot check cord fastened to Pup's collar. Move farther away from Pup on the stays. Make sure you always have a hand on the check cord to ensure his compliance. Again, keep the lesson brief. The more time you spend, the greater the probability that Pup will screw up and you'll have to correct him. We want these initial sessions to be short, sweet, and successful.

LESSON FOUR: THE NON-RETRIEVE

As I mentioned earlier, the non-retrieve is the backbone and foundation of a steady, calm hunting companion. Incorporate this training principle into your dog's life and you will produce a gun dog that is vastly superior in behavior and manners.

To begin, put Pup on the twenty-foot check cord and go through a couple of repetitions of the heel, sit, stay drills. Then tell Pup to sit. Walk about six feet from him. With your hand raised in the traffic cop gesture and your eyes glued on Pup, give an authoritative "sit" command. Next toss a dummy behind you so that Pup will have to run straight past you to retrieve it. Give the dummy a weak, low three-foot toss, which will make it much less tempting to Pup. You are engineering the situation so that Pup will be successful and you can reward him.

If Pup remains sitting, you've got it made. Tell him "sit" again, and slowly step out and pick up the dummy yourself. Then return to Pup and stroke him gently several times on the shoulders, the reward for the correct behavior sequence.

Go through this same sequence twice more, with you picking up the dummy.

The fourth time, let Pup retrieve the dummy. Send Pup with a snappy hand signal and the command "back." When he returns to you with the dummy, don't grab at it. Grasp Pup by the collar and pet him generously while the dummy is in his mouth. Then take it from him with the command "leave it."

Don't move toward Pup as he brings you the dummy. This will tend to cause him to either drop it or move away from you. If he shows any reluctance about bringing the dummy to you, simply back away from him.

If he drops the dummy on the way back, don't worry about it. The objective here is for him to retrieve the dummy and come back to you. Encourage him to come, and pet him when he gets to you. After the behavior becomes more solidly established, he will forget to drop the dummy.

The non-retrieve: Tell Pup to sit. Walk about six feet from him. With your hand in the traffic cop gesture, command "sit" again. Toss a dummy behind you so that Pup will have to run past you to retrieve it. Tell him "sit" again, then slowly step away and pick up the dummy yourself.

Finish the training session with one more non-retrieve, with you picking up the dummy. He should retrieve about one out of four dummies that he sees fall. This is a fairly good ratio to maintain during all of Pup's training sessions. Then he doesn't expect to retrieve every throw, and it will be much easier in the future for him to remain calm and steady while guns are shooting and birds are falling.

Lessons Five through Ten: Increasing the Distance

The next five sessions should be a continuation of the first four. You should repeat the same heeling, sitting, staying, and coming drills. Pup should be trailing a twenty- or thirty-foot check cord, so that you can get a hand or foot on it if necessary. The distance you move away from Pup during the staying sequences should increase gradually to fifty or sixty feet. Remember to walk all the way back to him occasionally, so that he doesn't get in the habit of always coming to you after staying.

The non-retrieve throw should be increased in three- to ten-foot increments, so that by lesson ten the dummy falls fifty to sixty feet away from you. Keep yourself in the habit of standing a few feet in front of Pup so that he will have to run right past you to break on a retrieve. That way it is much easier for him to keep himself sitting there while the oh-so-tempting dummy is falling out front.

When you and Pup have reached this point, you have taught him everything he needs to know to be a good gun dog. In these first ten lessons we have trained Pup to heel, sit, stay, and come on command. He is steady and doesn't retrieve until sent. We have even started him on hand signals. We've been sending him from several feet away with a hand signal. The non-retrieves have also planted the seed of calmness, which will make it easier to get him to stop on a whistle and take a hand signal in the future.

All that is required now is repeating these behaviors in the face of steadily increasing distraction and temptation. Also, we will steadily increase the distances involved.

CHAPTER 14

MARKED RETRIEVES

UP TO NOW you've heard more than enough about dog psychology, obedience, communication, etc. Undoubtedly, you and Pup want to get on with the retrieving. Marked retrieves, or retrieves that Pup sees fall, are great fun for Pup and you. Retrieving is also a behavior Pup is born with. It does not require a tremendous amount of training. Again, try to let him retrieve only 25 percent of the marks that he sees fall.

The major objectives in further training on marks are: (1) to build up Pup's skills at retrieving longer falls and (2) to develop his abilities on double and triple marked retrieves for those occasions when you knock down two or more birds. More important, multiple marks will be used to introduce Pup to lining, which will get him started on blind retrieves.

When there has been no shot and Pup has not seen anything fall, and you tell him to jump into that freezing water to get a bird that only you know about—then Pup really needs to believe that you're always right when you send him for a bird. To help develop Pup's faith in you, you work him on double and triple marks. He knows that second or third bird is out there, but his memory has faded somewhat and he needs a little faith in you to launch after it.

To further help Pup in launching for memory birds and blinds, be very consistent in the way you send him. Always line up his body so that he is pointing toward the bird you want. You can send him from your side with a hand extended over the top of his head and the command "back," giving him a line toward the bird. You can stand a step or two away from him and send him with a side cast and the command "fetch." Whichever method you choose, be consistent. Do it the same way every time. That way you develop a habit that will carry over to blind retrieves.

After lesson ten of obedience, you should be throwing the dummy out to your maximum throwing range. Here, again, you should be careful not to break the "Don't train in now what you have to train out later" rule. If you continue that same throwing distance for too long, Pup will get in the habit of hunting at your maximum throwing distance. And you will have to do some extra training to counteract that habit.

To increase the distance of your marks you have three choices:
1. Buy a dummy launcher. These come with three different loads to shoot three different distances. This is a good training aid, and if you mount it on a shoulder stock, it performs

the additional function of conditioning Pup to look where the gun points. Treat the dummy launcher just like a gun: Be careful to introduce Pup to it in a manner that ensures he won't be

A dummy launcher will help you propel the dummy beyond your maximum throwing range.

afraid of it. For the non-retrieves, walk out and pick up the dummy yourself, unless you are working more than one dog. In that case, Pup sits and honors while another dog picks up 75 percent of the dummies.

2. Enlist a helper to be your dummy thrower. The helper can walk out as far as you direct him to throw the dummy. He also saves you a lot of walking to pick up the non-retrieves.

3. Act as your own dummy thrower. Leave Pup sitting and walk out 10, 20, 30, or 150 yards, as the situation requires. This method of lengthening the throws calls for a lot of walking on your part, but it is my pick for the most effective method. The best marking and lining dogs I have had were trained with me going out to do all the throwing of marks and then walking back in to handle the dog.

In addition to stretching Pup out, you'll be starting him on double and triple marks. Note that you don't train Pup to do double retrieves by going out and throwing two dummies and testing to see how he does. These initial lessons should be structured so that he's always successful. You start with a single, repeat the single and add another mark to make it a double. This works on Pup's inclination to return with confidence to the location where he found the previous single mark. Also, in the interests of structuring for success, you should make the second mark at least ninety degrees away from the first. Then Pup won't get confused over which one he picked up first. Additionally, run the first few lessons in very light cover. A football field, golf course, or park is excellent. As Pup's proficiency and confidence grow, gradually move him to heavier cover.

❖

LESSON ONE

You and Pup have progressed to the point where he sits calmly while you throw a dummy when you're standing in front of him. Keep standing a few steps in front. This will continue to make it easy for Pup to be steady.

To make sure that Pup succeeds on his first double mark, work him in short grass so that he can easily see the dummies on the ground. To further ensure success, every memory bird will be retrieved first as a single.

1. Sit Pup and take a few steps out in front of him.
2. Throw a single dummy. Send Pup to retrieve it. When he returns with the dummy, take it from him and step back out in front of him.
3. Throw the dummy back to the same spot from which Pup just retrieved.
4. Turn and throw another dummy ninety degrees to the left of the first throw.
5. Let Pup sit a few seconds to practice his steadiness.
6. Send Pup. He will invariably go for the last dummy thrown.
7. When he returns, take the dummy. Have him heel and sit so that he is facing the memory bird. Send him for it.
8. After Pup completes this first double, throw it again. This time you walk out and pick up the dummies, or send another dog for them if you are working with friends.
9. Complete the lesson by giving Pup one more double, with the dummies thrown to the same places as the first double.

The marked retrieve: Toss out a dummy...

Let Pup retrieve it...

When he returns with the dummy, step back out in front of him. Throw another dummy to the same spot. Now toss a second dummy ninety degrees from the first one...

Send Pup for the last dummy thrown. When he returns, send him for the memory bird.

LESSON TWO

Up to now you have been working Pup at your maximum throwing distance. Now it's time to start stretching him out so that he doesn't get firmly entrenched in the habit of retrieving everything at that distance.

1. Sit Pup. Command him to stay. Walk out thirty or forty feet from him. Throw a dummy as far out as you can. Then go and pick it up yourself.
2. Walk out the same thirty or forty feet and throw another dummy as far as you can.
3. Walk back to Pup and send him for the dummy.
4. After Pup returns with the dummy, sit him back at the same spot. Walk out again and throw a repeat of the first single.
5. Walk over and throw another dummy so that it falls at least ninety degrees from the first fall and thirty or forty yards from Pup.
6. Walk in and send Pup on the retrieves. First send him for the last dummy thrown, since that's the one he going to want first. Then send him for the memory bird.
7. Finish the lesson by throwing the same two dummies again and leave pup sitting while you walk out and pick them up.

LESSONS THREE THROUGH TEN

Continue the double marks you started with lesson eleven. Progressively increase the distance until Pup is doing marked retrieves to 150 yards or more. Also, vary the training locations and work Pup in increasingly heavy cover. The key point in increasing the distances and degree of cover is to always keep it within Pup's capability. Again, you'll want to structure each training lesson so that Pup succeeds.

WATER

Pup should be getting some of these training sessions in the water. As a prerequisite, make sure he's been pleasantly introduced to the water (see chapter 17). Keep the lessons within his capability, and keep a few rocks handy on the early water work. When Pup is having trouble succeeding on a water retrieve, a rock thrown to splash near the desired dummy can turn failure into success. On longer water retrieves, a slingshot can help you fling the rocks that extra distance.

WORK SEVERAL DOGS TO PROMOTE STEADINESS

Picking up the required non-retrieves yourself can be a lot of work, especially on the longer throws. To save you the walking, it helps to work several dogs. Moreover, this practice will help promote steadiness in Pup.

Recruit two or three friends and their dogs to train with you. Then, at every training session, have all the dogs sit and honor the dog you're working as you run through the training exercise. Run each of the dogs through the session, one at a time. Work with them on the leash first, taking them off when they are trustworthy enough. The honoring dogs should be placed twenty feet or more away from the working dog so that it is easier for them to maintain self-control.

If you have two dogs, you can also work them by yourself. Here's how:

1. First, do the obedience drills in the yard and train the dogs to come when called by name. Get them proficient at heeling, sitting, and staying.

   Sit the dogs thirty feet apart and then give the traffic cop gesture to one while you call the other to you by name. Call the second dog to you by name.

   Start with the dogs on either side of you so that they are 180 degrees apart. Gradually move them closer together as they get used to coming individually when called. If your dogs live in the house, make them sit, then call them and have them come individually every time you bring them in from outside. When the dogs are coming when called, with each dog calmly awaiting his name before he comes, they are ready to be worked as a pair.

Working two dogs: Sit the dogs thirty feet apart. Give the traffic cop gesture to one while you call the other to you.

2. Now take the pair of dogs and sit them down twenty feet apart. Step out front of them about fifteen feet and throw out a dummy. Keep one dog in his place with the traffic cop gesture while you call the other over and send him for the dummy. Then repeat it but send the other dog for the dummy.

3. Over a period of several training sessions, move the dogs closer together until they are sitting right next to each other while you throw a dummy. Call one and send him while the other sits calmly and waits his turn.

CHAPTER 15

BLIND RETRIEVES

WHEN PUP DOESN'T SEE the bird fall, he will have to make a blind retrieve. You have to send him out toward the bird and direct him with hand signals. A blind retrieve requires a lot of training on your part and a lot of faith on Pup's.

There are two key points to remember about blind retrieves:

1. The more marks Pup picks up, the less inclined he is to learn to trust you to get him to the bird. Every marked retrieve trains him a little more in self-sufficiency. The more marked retrieves he gets in early training, the more difficult it will be to train him to take direction from you on blind retrieves.

   So start Pup on blinds and hand signals as soon as he is obedient and steady. That should be shortly after lesson ten of his obedience training. Don't wait until he's completed several hundred marked retrieves. Waiting just makes the training task more difficult.

2. Pup has a control distance. That control distance is the distance at which he will stop and take a cast from the handler. Early in Pup's training it will only be a few feet. The purpose of much of the subsequent training is to gradually move this control distance out 150 to 200 yards.

HOW MUCH

Casting drills and handling patterns are very repetitive and can become monotonous for Pup. You should match the frequency of lessons to your dog's activity level. If you have a high-energy dog, then three handling pattern lessons per week should be about right. For a lower energy dog, one or two sessions per week are plenty. Use a little judgment and discretion. If your dog starts to slow down or lose his enthusiasm on the handling pattern, give him a short break and decrease the frequency of lessons.

Ideally, you should intersperse these hand-signal lessons with Pup's obedience lessons, including non-retrieves. That way Pup will remain steady and enthusiastic.

THE HANDLING PATTERN

The foundation for blind retrieves is the handling pattern, which should be set up in a convenient place for you to work Pup regularly over a period of several weeks. The initial training on the handling pattern should be done in the same field, with the stations located in the same place for every training session. The lessons should run about ten to fifteen minutes, and you should be careful not to overdo it, especially in warm weather. Pup will be doing a lot of running on these handling lessons, so give him a few minutes between retrieves to catch his breath and cool off. Though not necessary, it is very helpful to take a lawn mower and mow the paths defining the handling pattern.

You can visualize the handling pattern in terms of a baseball diamond as diagrammed below. You will be sending Pup from home plate toward second base. You will be stopping him with a whistle blast at the pitcher's mound to cast him either left to third base, right to first base, or back to second base.

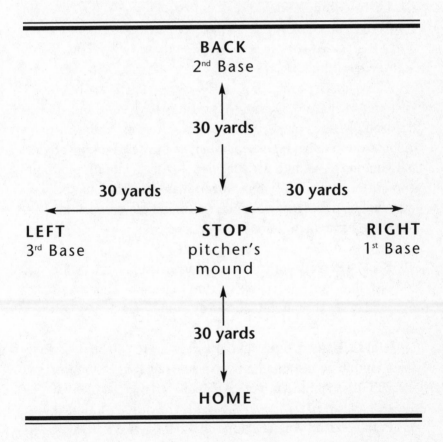

BACK
2nd Base

30 yards

30 yards   30 yards

LEFT   **STOP**   **RIGHT**
3rd Base   pitcher's   1st Base
      mound

30 yards

HOME

OVERVIEW

Training Pup on the handling pattern uses simple Pavlovian conditioning. The behaviors you will be training are:

1. Back—going out and away from you when sent.
2. Single whistle blast, or the command "sit"—stopping and sitting on whistle command.
3. Right—casting to the right.
4. Left—casting to the left.

HAND SIGNALS

If you want to tell a dog where to go, he must be looking at you, and you must give him a visual signal with plenty of motion in it. Additionally, the different directional signals should be separate and distinct from each other to minimize confusion.
The three hand signals are:

1. Back—Extend your hand and arm straight up, palm out, just like the traffic cop's "stop" gesture. This command sends Pup straight out and away from you.

2. Right—Extend your right arm fully to the right side. Take a simultaneous step or two in the same direction, as that will give Pup more motion to see.

3. Left—Extend your left arm fully to the left side. Take a step or two to give Pup a better visual cue to do what you want.

There are a couple of points that will make hand signals easier for you and Pup. Think about what Pup is seeing when you are giving that hand signal. If he is fifty yards away, and you are giving a lackadaisical hand signal with little motion and little differentiation between right and back, it can sometimes be difficult for Pup to understand what you are telling him to do. If you are wearing camouflage and standing where you blend in with the background, it can be very difficult for Pup to read your signals.

Therefore, make your signals separate and distinct. Take a couple of steps right or left with those casts to give Pup better visual signals. On back commands, stretch your arm fully to the vertical position so that Pup has the best opportunity to see it.

Back

Right

Left

A WORD ABOUT WHISTLES

You will be using a single whistle blast to signal Pup to stop and look to you for a directional hand signal. There are two kinds of whistles: those with peas and those without. The whistle with a pea sounds very loud to your ear, and it is loud to your ear. If you blow it energetically enough and frequently enough, it will damage your hearing.

Dogs hear a much higher frequency range than people. The whistles without peas, like the Acme model $210\frac{1}{2}$, are much softer on human ears, while carrying as far as any other whistle. In addition to preserving you and your hunting companions' hearing, the lower noise level makes hunting much more enjoyable.

You really don't need to make a lot of noise with a whistle in order for Pup to hear it. You would be amazed at how far out Pup can hear a simple verbal hiss. I frequently make a simple hissing sound, "Ssssss," to tell my dogs to stop, sit, and look at me. They can hear it quite well out to thirty yards or more.

One factor to be aware of in judging how well Pup should hear a whistle is how much noise he is making. If he is charging through shallow water with quite a bit of splashing, then it will be harder for him to hear you. Similarly, if Pup is charging through a field of dry cornstalks, he will be creating enough noise to make it difficult for him to hear you.

CASTING DRILLS

The first five lessons we will teach Pup are the component parts of the handling pattern, then we'll combine the pieces into the complete handling pattern. In order to make it easier for Pup, you should fix the location of this handling pattern and keep the dummies, stopping point, etc., in the same places.

LESSON ONE:

1. Take Pup to your fixed handling pattern and sit him at the pitcher's mound.
2. Walk over toward first base and throw two dummies to first base.
3. With Pup sitting at the pitcher's mound, walk back to home plate.
4. Blow a single blast.
5. When Pup looks at you, give the verbal command "right," accompanied by an emphatic hand signal to the right as you take a couple of steps in that direction.
6. After Pup brings you the dummy, put him back on the pitcher's mound and repeat the sequence for another right cast.
7. Next go through the same sequence for two left casts, sending Pup from the pitchers mound to third base.
8. Go through the same sequence for two back casts, standing at home plate and casting Pup back to second base.
9. Finally, leave Pup sitting at home plate while you walk out and toss two dummies on second base. Then walk back and send him to retrieve them. You may send him from the heel position or take a step or two away and send him with a casting motion. The critical matter here is to sit Pup so that his spine is aligned toward second base. That will cause him to head toward second base as opposed to first or third. Dogs nearly always take off in the direction that their backbone is aligned.

LESSON TWO:

1. Sit Pup at home plate and walk back and toss two dummies on second base.
2. Go back to home plate and send Pup twice to successively pick up the two dummies.
3. Repeat lesson one.

LESSONS THREE THROUGH FIVE

Repeat lesson two.

SIT-ON-WHISTLE DRILLS

While you are doing these casting drills at your handling pattern location, you should throw in a few "sit" drills in the back yard. These should be semi-play sessions.

Pup can learn a lot through "play." The sit-on-whistle drills will prepare him for taking hand signals when you send him on a blind retrieve.

Walk around in the yard with Pup. When Pup gets out away from you several feet, give a whistle blast and command "sit." Immediately after Pup sits, praise him. Then quickly throw a dummy for him to retrieve and let him break to retrieve it. Do this exercise in the yard several times a week while moving the sit distance farther from you.

THE HANDLING PATTERN: PUTTING THE PIECES TOGETHER

After the first five lessons of casting drills, Pup should be ready to put the pieces together. As Pup starts on the handling pattern, you will be requiring him to go out, stop on command, and take a cast. In order to ensure that Pup is under control, attach a fifty-foot check cord to his collar and let him drag it. A ¼-inch polypropylene water-ski-type rope works great for this purpose, as it is lightweight and low in friction when it drags. It also floats for water work.

A very important but subtle point: Always give Pup some positive reinforcement for stopping on the whistle. Every time you stop him and have him sit, give him verbal praise. Then give him the directional cast.

In lessons six through fifteen you will be sending Pup toward second base, stopping him at the pitcher's mound, and casting him right, left, or back. Initially you will be sending Pup from a point partway between home plate and the pitcher's mound. You need to initially stop Pup within the length of his check cord—this ensures that the desired behavior sequence occurs. (Actually, it would be wise to initially stop Pup within six to ten feet of you, as that will probably be his control distance. As he gets better at stopping on the pitcher's mound, you can gradually start backing up in ten-foot increments until you are sending him from home plate, stopping him for a cast on the pitcher's mound.)

LESSON SIX

1. Sit Pup three quarters of the way from home plate to the pitcher's mound.
2. Walk around and toss two dummies on first base, and two dummies on third. Walk partway toward second and throw six dummies on second base.
3. Walk back to Pup. Making sure his backbone is aligned with second base, send him toward second.
4. When Pup is six to ten feet away from you, stop him with a "sit" command, a whistle blast, or a loud hiss. Then give him a back cast to continue on to second base to retrieve a dummy.
5. Repeat this sequence, stopping Pup a little farther away and giving him another back cast to second base.
6. Send Pup, stop him on the pitcher's mound, and send him right to first base.
7. Send Pup, stop him on the pitcher's mound, and send him left to third base.
8. Send Pup, stop him on the pitcher's mound, and send him back to second base.
9. Send Pup, stop him on the pitcher's mound, and send him right to first base.
10. Send Pup, stop him on the pitcher's mound, and send him left to third base.
11. Send Pup, stop him on the pitcher's mound, and send him back to second base.
12. End the lesson by sending Pup up the middle from home plate to second base twice without stopping him.

LESSON SEVEN

Repeat lesson six. Pup's control distance should be getting longer, so run Pup from a point halfway between home plate and the pitcher's mound. If Pup is not stopping well, shorten up the distance and occasionally put your foot on that check cord.

If Pup doesn't stop on command, put your foot on the check cord and make him stop.

LESSON EIGHT

Repeat lesson seven. Pup should be stopping well enough that you can run him from home plate.

LESSONS NINE THROUGH FIFTEEN

Repeat lesson seven, running Pup from home plate.

POPPING

Pup will probably start popping. Again, popping is great. Popping occurs when Pup stops and looks to you for a hand signal without your giving the whistle signal. Popping indicates that Pup has figured out what you are doing and is looking to you for the next hand signal. A dog that pops about every thirty yards on a blind retrieve is perfect for hunting. You don't have to make any noise by blowing the whistle. When Pup pops, tell him he's a good dog and give him the directional cast he is looking for.

❖

PUP DOESN'T GO THE WAY YOU SEND HIM

Sometimes you will line up Pup for second base and he will take off toward first or third base. Don't worry about it. Directional lining is not very important for a hunting dog.

Stopping and taking a cast is the important function for a hunting dog. When you are trying to line Pup up in the middle of the pattern and he runs up the first base line, let him go a few yards. Let him go halfway to first base. Then stop him with a whistle or "sit" command. Cast him to the pitcher's mound, where you stop him and give him another cast to the base of your preference.

❖

PUP TAKES THE WRONG CAST

Occasionally, when you say go left, Pup is going to go right. Your appropriate reaction is to quickly stop Pup and give him the left cast again. The faster you stop him the more easily he will be persuaded to go left on the second cast. You should not let him travel more than three steps when he takes off in the wrong direction. Stopping him quickly will make Pup much more likely to go the right way on the second cast.

CAUTION ON HEAT

When you are putting Pup through his paces on the handling pattern, remember that he is doing a tremendous amount of running in a very short time, while you are simply standing there giving commands. It is very easy for Pup to get overheated in hot, humid weather. Be careful. If it's hot, run Pup early in the morning. Give him a few minutes of rest between retrieves so he can cool down a bit. Wet Pup down before you start the pattern exercise. Put your handling pattern next to a lake so he can jump in the water and cool off a few times during the hot-weather training sessions.

COLD BLINDS AND CONTROL DISTANCE

After Pup has had those first fifteen handling lessons he is ready to run some cold blinds. A cold blind is when you have planted the blind ahead of time and Pup has no idea that anything is out there in the field. Don't try any shortcuts here. It is essential that Pup be able to run handling patterns before you start him on cold blinds.

Leave Pup in the car while you walk out and hide two dummies. Twenty yards is plenty of distance to begin with, as you want to keep Pup within his control distance. Don't walk straight back from the dummies to the point from which you will run Pup. If you do, Pup will soon train himself to simply track you by your scent. This is a great way to train a tracking dog, but it is counterproductive to directional training.

After the two dummies are planted, snap a thirty-foot check cord to Pup's collar. Let him drag it for several lessons until you are confident that he is under control.

1. Sit Pup facing in the general direction of the dummies and send him.
2. Start walking after him immediately, so that you minimize the distance between you and Pup.
3. Let him get about twenty feet away and command him to sit with either your voice or whistle.
4. If he doesn't stop, step on the check cord.
5. When he stops and looks at you, give him a hand signal toward the dummy.
6. Immediately after Pup takes the cast, continue walking toward him, again the objective being to keep him within his control distance.
7. Stop Pup again after he has gone twenty or thirty feet. Give him another cast.
8. You should try to have Pup succeed in getting the dummy in two or three casts so that the reward is linked to the behavior of stopping and taking casts. Be sure to send Pup to the downwind side of the dummy so he can smell it.
9. After Pup retrieves one dummy, take him back to the starting point and send him back for the other dummy as a confidence builder. Stop him once on the way so that control is maintained.

For several weeks, gradually increase the length of Pup's cold blinds. Also, keep running him on the handling pattern. A good mix is 50 percent of each. The cold blinds should be in light cover initially. As Pup gets more under control, gradually work into heavier cover. The heavier the cover, the more difficult it will be to keep Pup under control.

CORRECTION FOR NOT STOPPING

When Pup starts disobeying the whistle command to sit on blind retrieves, it is usually for one of the following reasons:

1. Testing instead of training. You are experimenting to see how far Pup can go and still be under control. If you do this often you will be training Pup to disobey. Only blow the "sit" whistle when Pup is going to stop—that is, inside his control distance. Don't try to move that distance out too rapidly. Move it at Pup's pace, not yours.

2. Too many marks, not enough handling. When Pup is getting a lot of marked retrieves and only a little work on the handling pattern, then he is going to become much less responsive to the whistle on blind retrieves. Remember that every marked retrieve that Pup finds on his own makes him a little less ready to look to you for help on blind retrieves. After Pup has started running the handling pattern, he needs very few marked retrieves.

3. During hunting season, Pup is probably getting too many marked retrieves and practically no work on the handling pattern. This combination will cause Pup to become progressively less responsive to the whistle. The solution is to run Pup more on the handling pattern to compensate for the overabundance of marked retrieves he gets during hunting season.

Even better, turn some of those marked retrieves into blind retrieves. If you are duck hunting, don't send Pup every time a duck hits the water. If the duck is dead and not being carried off by wind or current, leave it lying. Wait till you've killed your limit, and then let Pup do the retrieving. Having to wait half an hour or an hour or more will make Pup much less sure of the locations of the downed ducks. He will much more readily look to you for help. Additionally, the waiting will keep him steadier.

Since very few of us dog trainers do everything the theoretically correct way, there will be instances when Pup will disobey the "stop" whistle and the trainer needs to give some correction. Walk out and grab Pup. Pick him up clear off the ground and give him a shake. Sit him and walk away. Stop within his control distance and continue handling him to the blind.

When you find him disobeying with any frequency, look at the overall program. You are probably giving Pup too many marks and not enough sessions on the handling pattern. Increasing his work on the handling pattern is the best solution for poor performance at stopping on the whistle.

Another strategy that helps keep Pup under control is maintaining the bluff. Try to only blow the "sit" whistle when Pup is likely to obey. When he's 100 yards away, charging through knee-deep water, headed straight as an arrow toward something he thinks is a duck, don't blow the whistle. Wait till he's found out that his objective is not a duck. Then when he has slowed down and his course starts wavering, blow the whistle. Pup is much more likely to stop then.

Never quit running Pup on the handling pattern. The key to a good handling dog is more pattern work and fewer marks.

CHAPTER 16

INTRODUCING PUP TO GUNS, DECOYS, ETC.

THE KEY TO introductions is to make them pleasant. When Pup is being introduced to new experiences or objects, it is the trainer's responsibility to make sure that Pup doesn't develop any negative associations with the new place or thing being introduced.

The most important introductions are to water, guns, decoys, birds, and boats. The introduction to water is treated in the next chapter, which covers water training. The other introductions will be dealt with here.

GUNS

The essential points on introducing Pup to the sound of a shotgun are (1) plan the introduction so that the noise is gradually increasing in volume and (2) make sure the noise is associated with the activity that Pup loves best: retrieving.

Save the gun introduction until Pup is working well on marked retrieves and has done some water work. You will need a friend with a dog to help on the gun introduction. Find a lake or pond where your friend can work his dog on water retrieves while you and Pup stand and watch from at least 150 yards away. Use a 20-gauge or 12-gauge shotgun and use light field loads.

Your friend should work his dog on two or three short water retrieves as Pup watches. When Pup is thoroughly intrigued and excited by all the activity accompanying the dummy throws— the splashing and retrieving—your friend should add a shot as he throws the dummy.

If the shot doesn't bother Pup, move him closer at whatever rate he feels comfortable. After several shots, you and Pup should be standing next to your friend, and Pup should have developed the best of associations with gunshots. Give Pup a couple of retrieves accompanied by gunshots.

A proper introduction to the gun should last a lifetime. If, however, a dog gets gun-shy subsequent to the proper gun introduction, then it is probably because he had his ears "rung" by muzzle blast. If Pup gets out in front the muzzle blast from your shotgun, it will hurt him and will certainly contribute to early deafness.

DECOYS

The introduction to decoys is a piece of cake. All you have to do is teach Pup to expect to find dummies and ducks out past the decoys. Simply put out a dozen decoys and throw a dummy well past them. Send Pup for the retrieve. If he gets distracted by the decoys, throw another dummy or throw a rock and make a splash out where you want him to go.

Even after proper introduction and lots of work with decoys, Pup still might retrieve a decoy the first time he goes duck hunting. Don't worry about it. It's excitement and confusion over a new situation. If Pup retrieves a decoy, simply take it from him and throw a rock to make a splash near the duck.

The basic point here is that after Pup has picked up a few ducks out past the decoys, then decoys will no longer be interesting to him.

BIRDS

Pup's introduction to birds should occur after he has had plenty of work on dummies.

Instill the habit of retrieving to hand, and have it firmly established before giving Pup birds. Then if Pup happens to have some tendency to be hard mouthed, the delivery habits built up with dummies will probably override the hard-mouth tendency and you will have no problem.

© Chuck Petrie

Once Pup has picked up a few birds beyond the decoys, the dekes will no longer interest him.

What if Pup does crunch the bird when you introduce it? The easiest solution is:

1. Make sure Pup is not hungry. Start feeding him in the mornings so that he has a full stomach when you work him.
2. Use ducks. They are big and take some work and time for Pup to eat.
3. Work in the water. When he is swimming, Pup can't stop to eat a duck.

The above steps should work on dogs that have only a slight tendency to hard mouth. This trait has a strong hereditary link and is difficult to eradicate with training. If you have a dog that really tears into birds with gusto, then your life will be a lot more pleasant if you find him a good non-hunting home and get yourself another dog.

BOATS

Ideally, you should introduce Pup to a boat before his first duck hunt. That first hunt is confusing enough, so remove one of the variables by getting Pup comfortable in a boat. The boat introduction is one of the easiest.

Put a boat in the water. Put a leash on Pup and take him to the boat. You get in first and then gently lead Pup in with plenty of verbal encouragement and support. After he's in, pet him a little and then take him for a boat ride. If the boat doesn't bother Pup, you have accomplished your goal.

If Pup shows signs of uneasiness in the boat, give him a few more rides over the next few days. When Pup is comfortable in the boat, the lesson is finished.

Boat introductions are as simple as getting Pup used to sitting in the boat, then taking him for a pleasant ride across the lake or pond.

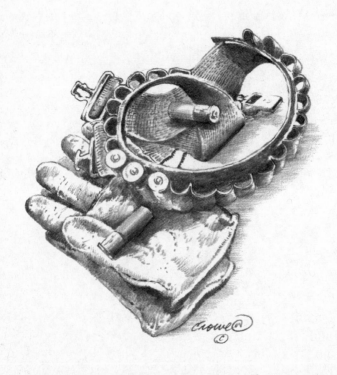

CHAPTER **17**

WATER TRAINING

RETRIEVERS ARE BORN loving water; your job is to ensure that you don't teach yours not to love it. The best philosophy is to get Pup trained on land, where you can control the outcome. After Pup is reliable on land, then go to the water. The key is developing his confidence. If you train Pup well on land and develop his confidence in the water, those trained behaviors will transfer well to water.

INTRODUCTION TO WATER

The easiest water introduction for puppies occurs when you have a whole litter that is seven to eight weeks old and it is summertime. Find part of the lake or pond where the bank gently slopes. Put on your boots or tennis shoes and take the litter of puppies for a walk. Walk them around on land for a while so that they get very warm. Then walk into the water. They will follow you and will probably automatically swim without ever missing a stroke. Puppies at this age have a natural inclination to swim and will do so automatically. However, be very careful not to try this in the winter. Putting a small puppy in cold water will simply teach him not to like water.

If Pup is born in fall or winter, he may be several months old before you introduce him to water. Or you may have acquired an older puppy that has missed an early introduction to water, or a pup that has had a bad introduction to water. In any case, the rules for Pup's introduction to water are the same:

1. Pick a gently sloping bank.
2. Do it in warm weather.
3. If you are throwing a dummy, make the first toss just long enough that Pup can get it by putting only his front feet in the water the first time. Then lengthen the toss a foot at a time until he is swimming.

Let Pup go in at his pace. Reward whatever small progress he makes. This is not a test, and there is no time limit. If Pup sticks one foot in, praise him. If he continues to be uneasy in the water, wade in with him. The object of initial water training is to do what is needed for Pup to learn that water is fun.

If Pup misses the window of opportunity for the swimming instinct to kick in, he may have trouble learning to swim. He may keep trying to climb out of the water, or persist in slapping the water with his front feet while his rear feet don't do much paddling. The solution is to get his front end down, which will level him out and cause him to swim naturally.

One tool that helps is the large plastic dummy. This dummy is heavy enough that Pup tires more quickly and gets that front end down so that he begins swimming naturally. Another strategy is to wade into the water with Pup and gently hold him by the collar while putting an arm under his belly to keep his rear end up. After he's made a few strokes in the proper orientation, the swimming instinct will usually kick in.

BANK RUNNING IS GREAT

Not letting a retriever run the bank is another widespread practice that can cause trouble in water training. As I mentioned earlier, bank running is a natural and desirable trait in a hunting dog.

Field trials have produced the fiction that bank running is bad. This is totally untrue. A dog's natural inclination is to take the fastest route. We should listen to Mother Nature and let the dog take the dry route on a retrieve. If you take staying in the water to its logical conclusion, you end up with a hypothermic dog.

The retriever's ultimate function is to retrieve ducks in cold water. The longer that retriever stays in the water, the more body heat he loses, and the fewer retrieves he will be able to make before he succumbs to hypothermia, which can kill him. Conversely, the more time he is running on land, the more heat he is generating by the metabolism of his large muscles. Thus it is desirable for a retriever to run the bank whenever possible.

WATER TRAINING

The cardinal rules of water training are:

1. Don't train in the water when the water is cold. An artificial dummy waiting at the end of a long freezing swim is not enough reward to keep Pup motivated about the water. If you absolutely can't restrain yourself from training Pup in cold weather, use birds. The best practice is to do the water training in warm weather and to take Pup hunting in cold weather.

Introducing Pup to water: On a warm day, lead him to a gently sloping bank...

Toss a dummy far enough that Pup can get it by just putting his feet in the water...

Pup's steps will be tentative at first, but that's OK. Let him go at his own pace...

Lengthen the toss a foot at a time, and...Pup will be swimming before he even knows it.

2. Train Pup well on land first, then take him to the water.

Again, the most valuable tool for water training is a pocket full of rocks. When Pup can't find the dummy or bird, wait till he looks at you and then throw a rock so that it makes a splash near the dummy or bird. The rock throwing will also help Pup learn hand signals in the water.

MARKS

Assuming the weather is warm enough, start Pup on water work after he is steady on double marks on land. Start out by requiring him to be steady on the water. Pup will have a tendency to be less steady on water because it is generally more exciting to him.

The other thing that makes it difficult for Pup to be steady on water is the fact that you can't walk on water. It is much harder for you to pick up the dummies on water. Water work is where you really need to join several friends for joint training sessions. Ideally, get three other dogs at the working session so that your dog gets to retrieve only 25 percent of the falls. That way he will get enough non-retrieves to keep him steady.

The other tendency on water training is to train Pup to hunt at a fixed distance—namely, your maximum throwing range. Again, the power of repetition will soon form a strong habit in Pup. He will be very good on dummies inside your throwing distance, but will fail on longer retrieves.

There are several techniques to gain greater distance:

1. Use the wind. Work from the side of the lake that puts the wind at your back. Throw two or three dummies out in a close bunch. Send Pup. During the time he's retrieving the first dummy, numbers two and three will have been blown out some distance. Similarly, during the time Pup is retrieving the second dummy, the third will have drifted a good bit farther. This drill will add distance to Pup's retrieving skills.

2. Use a dummy launcher. This tool comes with light, medium, and heavy loads to add distance to the retrieves.

3. Leave Pup sitting and walk around the pond to the other side and throw out a couple of dummies. Walk back and send Pup across. You might need to throw him a short one to establish the right entry spot into the water.

WATER ENTRY

Everybody likes to see a retriever take a long, flying leap into the water. However, flying leaps are not always healthy for Pup. If you hunt in cypress bottoms where there are plenty of cypress knees lurking just beneath the water's surface, a flying water entry can result in a massive puncture wound to the chest. The same applies to many manmade lakes, where old tree trunks may lurk just below the water's surface.

Moreover, the wish to produce a flying leap water entry sometimes contributes to an unsteady dog, because the easiest way to produce that dramatic entry is to get Pup all revved up.

Blind Retrieves in Water

The key to water blinds is getting Pup to believe that there is a bird out there even though he didn't see it fall. You instill this confidence by making sure Pup is successful at every retrieve.

Start with short blinds that Pup can readily see floating on the water, and then gradually lengthen them. Program Pup to expect to find birds and dummies out in the water.

When he's swimming out after a mark, far enough out that he won't hear the splash, toss out a short dummy as a blind. After he returns with the mark, send him for the short blind. Gradually make them longer. The more dummies he finds out in the water, the more prone he'll be to jump in the water and look even when he has not seen one fall.

Stopping on the Whistle in the Water

Before you try stopping Pup in the water, he should be perfect on land. In his early water work, make sure Pup is close when you blow the whistle. His control distance is much shorter in the water than on land. Keep a pocket full of rocks handy. By throwing a rock, you can ensure that he is successful in getting the blind retrieve in one or two casts.

The key to training Pup to stop on the whistle consistently in the water is to blow it when Pup is likely to stop. During early training, stop him close. Always try to refrain from blowing the whistle when Pup is charging out with great purpose and appears to know where he is going. Wait until his course starts wavering, showing that he is unsure of his destination. Then blow the whistle. He will be much more likely to stop.

HUNTING IN WATER

The general rule for hunting Pup in water is to try and make it pleasant and comfortable. Don't hunt Pup in freezing conditions until he's two years old. Younger dogs are simply not tough and do not stand up to harsh conditions as well as older dogs.

When you do hunt Pup, make sure he has a place to get out of the water. Cold water acts like a heat sink, sucking the body heat out of a dog. Too much time in cold water can make Pup hypothermic and can kill him.

The neoprene dog vest is an excellent product to help keep your dog warm on cold hunting trips. This is especially true for dogs that live in the house and are thus not fully acclimated to cold weather.

Keep Pup under control. Again, whatever you allow him to do is what you are training him to do. If he's not trained well enough to be fully under control, keep him on a leash.

One of the best training aids is a four-foot piece of thin plastic-coated wire cable with a swivel snap attached to either end. You can get the components at a hardware or boat supply store. This piece of cable rolls up small and light, so you can keep it in the pocket of your hunting coat. The purpose of the steel in the cable is to prevent Pup from biting through it. Snap one end to the duck blind and the other to Pup's collar.

One way to make Pup steady, plus develop his blind retrieve proficiency, is to have him wait a good while before retrieving. If the duck you just shot is not crippled and not being carried off by wind or current, then leave it lying where it is. Wait until you've shot most or all of your limit before sending Pup to retrieve. This practice is an extension of the non-retrieves you gave Pup in training. It will continue to train him to be steady.

The added value of this practice is that it greatly speeds up Pup's proficiency at blind retrieves. If you shoot six or eight ducks or more over time, Pup isn't going to remember exactly where they are. He will know they are out there and thus will readily bail into the water, but he won't remember the exact location of all of them. He will more readily look to you for help than when he is immediately sent every time a duck falls.

If Pup is not fully proficient on hand signals, a bucket of rocks in the boat or blind will come in handy. If you can't get him to go where you want with a hand signal, throw a rock and he will head for the splash.

There is one problem that you should anticipate as Pup gains more hunting experience. Most of the birds that Pup retrieves will fall within 30 to 40 yards. Pup will get in the habit of hunting at that distance, and may have trouble getting out far enough to retrieve that long-sailing bird that falls at 150 yards. Thus Pup's training should include some water work on longer retrieves to keep him sharp in that area.

❖

CHAPTER 18

FORCE-FETCH
TRAINING

FORCE-FETCH TRAINING is training Pup to fetch a dummy, bird, or other object on command.

Only force-fetch train if and when you have to. If Pup delivers to hand naturally, reinforce and reward that behavior. Don't do things that cause Pup to change that behavior, and you may never have to force train him.

The two behaviors that may require you to force-fetch train are (1) dropping birds or dummies and (2) handling birds with a hard mouth. Neither behavior requires an immediate resorting to force training. With both, you are better served to wait on the force-fetch training.

DELIVERY TO HAND

The simplest way to ensure delivery to hand is to never let Pup get started in dropping dummies. Many pups are born with a tendency to deliver to hand but are inadvertently "trained" to drop the dummy on the way to the handler. There are several ways for this to happen, as well as several ways to prevent it:

1. **Wrong way:** You grab at the dummy as Pup comes up to you, and startle him, causing him to drop the dummy.

   Right way: Don't grab at the dummy. Crouch down and slip your hand under Pup's chin as he comes up. Help him hold the dummy in his mouth and stroke his head and praise him a couple of minutes as he holds the dummy. Then take it from him.

Each time Pup retrieves a dummy, help him hold it in his mouth while you stroke his head and praise him. Soon he will be holding it on his own.

2. **Wrong way:** You jump at Pup as he's coming and cause him to run from you.

   Right way: Puppies have an innate behavior to chase and be chased. Use the former. Move away from Pup a step or two as he comes up to you with the dummy.

Puppies have an innate desire to chase and be chased. Don't lunge at Pup when he's coming with the dummy. Instead, take a step or two back and trigger his urge to come to you.

3. **Wrong way:** Pup runs for the bushes with the dummy, you chase and catch him, he spits it out somewhere along the way.

   Right way: For several weeks, practice all subsequent retrieves in a place with no escape exits. A long hallway in the house is excellent. Develop the habit of delivery to hand before you venture near bushes again.

4. **Wrong way:** Pup comes to you with the dummy and you start harassing him to heel and sit to deliver. He starts dropping the dummy or stops coming to you, or both.

   Right way: Attach a six-foot length of cord to Pup's collar.

When Pup comes to you with the dummy, crouch down and slip your hand under his chin to hold the dummy in his mouth as you stroke his head and praise him. Then take the dummy from him, and with the check cord guide him to the heel position and command "sit" with a pull upward on the cord. After he sits, pet and praise him. After a number of repetitions, Pup will be heeling and sitting automatically when you've taken the dummy. Next, just reverse the sequence. When he comes up, don't take the dummy until after he has heeled and sat. He will be so much in the habit of heeling and sitting that he won't drop the dummy.

5. **Wrong way:** You use plastic dummies instead of the canvas kind.
   Right way: Use canvas dummies. Plastic dummies are slippery when wet, and less comfortable for a dog to carry than canvas dummies. Dogs are more likely to drop plastic dummies than canvas ones. Using plastic dummies increases the probability of encountering problems with Pup delivering to hand.

HARD MOUTH

If your dog is hard mouthed and rough on birds, simply train him with dummies for several months until he is obedient, steady, and capable of doing double marks and blind retrieves with confidence. Check him on birds again after that period of working strictly on dummies. Often, force of habit will prevail, and the hard mouth will be overridden by the strong habit of retrieving dummies softly to hand.

Force-Fetch Training: When to Do It

On the other hand, sometimes the hard mouth is still operating. Taking Pup through a thorough course of force-fetch training will usually cure it. Cease all other training for a couple of weeks while the force-fetch training is in progress. In the case of the hard-mouthed dog, you should condition Pup using a dowel, dummies, and birds. After the dowel and dummies, you should force him to fetch frozen birds first, then unfrozen birds.

For the dog that is dropping dummies, the solution is similar. If he's dropping them within a few feet of you, simply ignore it and continue with his initial obedience and retrieving work. After he's had several weeks of obedience work and is steady and doing double marks with confidence, start the force training. Cease all other work with Pup while you are engaged in the force-fetch training process.

If Pup is dropping birds far away from you, move his work to the water for a couple of weeks. Usually a dog won't spit a dummy while he's swimming with it. He will generally wait until he's exiting at water's edge to drop it. Therefore, give the distant dropper his retrieves in the water. The basic principle here is that you want a dog to have some foundation of obedience training and retrieving work before you put him through the force-training process.

Force Fetch as Foundation for Field-Trial Lining

Force-fetch training is done on nearly all field-trial dogs in America because of the importance of lining in field-trialing. If you don't plan on running field trials, and your dog delivers to hand and is gentle with birds, then you do not need to force-fetch train him.

If you are going to run field trials and want to win, then you should force-fetch train Pup. Force-fetch training is the foundation behavior for lining and is a necessary first step for forcing Pup on lines.

THE HIDDEN DANGER IN FORCE-FETCH TRAINING

The hidden danger in force-fetch training is that it compensates for behaviors that should be developed by selective breeding. I discovered this after a few years of working with many puppies of American field-trial breeding and many puppies of British field-trial breeding. There is a glaring behavioral difference between the two genetic pools. A much higher percentage of British puppies automatically delivers to hand.

You don't have to look far to find the reason. The British very seldom force-fetch train their dogs. This training practice is not widely accepted or practiced in England. Therefore, in that breeding population, soft mouth and delivery to hand are developed by selective breeding. Dogs that are not soft mouthed or that don't deliver to hand are not successful field dogs, and thus tend not to be hunted or campaigned in field trials. They also tend not to be bred as good working stock. In England, selective breeding is still operating to produce soft-mouthed retrievers.

In the U.S. working retriever population, training is used to produce soft-mouthed retrievers. Selective breeding for soft mouth and delivery to hand has been replaced by training to develop these traits.

Since force training has become a general and nearly universal practice in the training of field-trial dogs, we are camouflaging one of the major traits that molded the retrieving breeds through selective breeding of hundreds of generations. When you cover up a primary trait with training, it no longer has value for selective breeding. Today, when you look at a prospective sire for breeding, you can't tell whether his soft mouth and delivery to hand came from his ancestors or from his trainer.

One of the primary traits for which retrievers have been selectively bred is delivering an undamaged bird gently to hand. With the widespread practice of force-fetch training we have effectively reversed years and years of breeding selection.

FORCE-FETCH TRAINING: THE MECHANICS

Force-fetch training is bad for the breed, but we seem to be saddled with it. More and more sportsmen are having to force-fetch train their dogs to compensate for the lack of breeding selection. Force-fetch training appears to be a necessary evil.

Force-fetch training is a negative-conditioning process wherein the fetch behavior is an escape response. The negative stimulus that Pup is escaping in this case is an ear pinch or toe pinch. The sequence is:

SIGNAL	NEGATIVE STIMULUS	ESCAPE RESPONSE	REWARD
"Fetch"	Ear or Toe Pinch	Grab Dowel in Mouth	Stroked slowly and gently on head and top of neck and given gentle verbal praise

That describes the total conditioning sequence. For the best results, with the least amount of force, the sequence should be carefully structured and progressively built. The whole program can be completed in as few as three or four ten-minute sessions, or as many as fifteen or twenty. A lot depends on the nature of the individual dog. A lot more depends on the skill and experience level of the person doing the training.

The ear pinch method of force-fetch training, though simpler and faster for the skillful trainer, is not recommended for the novice trainer, who nearly always uses too much force.

EAR OR TOE PINCH, GROUND OR TABLE

There are two places and two methods to do the force-fetch training. You can do it on a table using the toe pinch, or you can do it on the ground using the ear pinch. If you are a fairly skillful dog trainer and have a cooperative dog, train on the ground using the ear pinch. This method is simpler, and faster for a skillful trainer. I have used both methods extensively. I prefer the ear pinch on the ground because it is simpler and faster. I have also watched a large number of novice trainers attempt the force-training process on the ground and have seen a lot of lost tempers, and confusion on the part of the dog and trainer. Generally, the novice trainer attempting to force-fetch train on the ground will nearly always use too much force and hamper the process.

For the novice trainer, the toe pinch method, with the dog on the table, works best.

If you are a novice trainer, make it easy on yourself and your dog. The toe pinch, with a dog up on a table, is the preferred method. It is more complicated and takes longer, but it is also much harder to screw up.

Tethering Pup up on the table puts you in complete control and makes it much easier for you to elicit the desired response from Pup at the right time. Putting Pup on a table for force-fetch training also accomplishes several other objectives:

1. It puts Pup in an unfamiliar place, which gives you an advantage.
2. It removes you from physical contact with Pup. It is much easier for you to maintain an objective attitude and keep your emotions out of the picture. Thus a training session is much less likely to devolve into a wrestling match.
3. It puts you in a comfortable position. You are less likely to lose patience.

BUILDING THE BEHAVIOR CHAIN

For the toe pinch method, start with the table. A four-by-eight sheet of plywood is a good size. Make it waist high and sturdy enough to support Pup. String a cable lengthwise about three feet above the table. The cable will initially serve to anchor Pup while allowing him to move back and forth the length of the table. Then you begin a step-by-step behavior-building process.

1. Pup must learn to give to pressure to the collar on his neck. Since you have already obedience trained Pup, he will have learned to give to his neck.

2. Put Pup on the table and let him get comfortable on it. Anchor Pup to the cable with a few swivel snaps fastened together. Tie him short enough so that he is in the sitting position. Walk him back and forth on the table a few times while petting and encouraging him. Get him comfortable on the table.

3. The next step is to make him accept a foreign object in his mouth. First make him accept your hand. If you don't like dog saliva, put on a leather glove.

First, get Pup to accept your hand. While holding his head steady with your left hand, take your right hand and put it in his mouth, grasping his lower jaw. He will quit fighting and relax after a few minutes.

    a. Grab Pup's collar with your left hand and hold his head still.

    b. Put your right hand in his mouth, grasping his lower jaw. Pup will probably resist this, but hold his collar firmly with your left hand while keeping the right one in his mouth. Talk calmly to him. He will quit fighting and relax after a few minutes. When he's relaxed, you know he has accepted your hand in his mouth. Then keep your right hand in his mouth and stroke him on the head with your left hand while praising him.

    c. Put your hand back in his mouth a couple of times and pet him with your free hand.

4. After Pup has accepted your hand, the next step is to have him accept a dowel. Use a six-inch-long piece of one-inch dowel.

a. Grasp Pup's collar with your left hand and hold him still.

b. Put the piece of dowel in his mouth. Hold his lower jaw till he accepts the dowel and relaxes. Then stroke his head and praise him while dowel is still in his mouth. You may need to use your left thumb to keep his jaw supported and the dowel in his mouth while you are petting him.

c. Repeat this four or five times.

Grasp Pup by the collar and put the dowel in his mouth.

5. Proceed to the toe pinch.

a. Attach a 24-inch length of ⅛-inch cord to Pup's front leg with a clove hitch just above the ankle joint. Run a half hitch around his middle two toes. Pull gently on the cord so that it pinches his toes. Use just enough pressure to make Pup uncomfortable enough to want to do something about it. Simultaneously, hold the dowel in front of his mouth. If he opens his mouth a little, push the dowel in. When the dowel goes in his mouth, the pinch should cease. Make him hold the dowel while you pet and praise him. If he doesn't open his mouth, use your dowel hand to open his mouth a little by pressing his jowl against his teeth with your index finger. As his mouth comes open a little, put the dowel in his mouth. As soon as the dowel is in his mouth, release the pinch. Make him hold the dowel while you pet and praise him.

b. If Pup is not reaching for the dowel when you pinch, or not opening his mouth, use more time—not more force. Hold the pinch a little longer, with the same intensity. Pry open his mouth, insert the dowel, and pet and praise him. Generally, more repetitions will get the job done.

c. Repeat the sequence until Pup is predictably reaching for the dowel upon feeling the pinch.

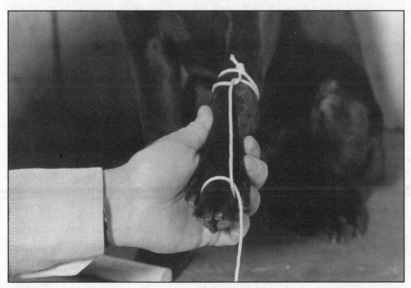

With the toe pinch method, a cord tied to Pup's leg and toes provides just enough pressure to make him want to do something about it—namely, hold the dowel, which causes the pressure to cease.

When Pup is automatically reaching for the dowel as he feels the pinch, it's time to add the command "fetch."

    a. With Pup on table, give a light pinch with the cord and command "fetch" as the dowel goes in Pup's mouth. Repeat several times.

    b. Lengthen the attachment from Pup's collar to the trolley cable, so that he reaches farther to grab the dowel. Repeat several times until Pup is taking the dowel just above the tabletop.

    c. Wrap some tape around each end of the dowel so that it has a dumbbell shape and the taped ends hold the dowel off the table. Require Pup to fetch it off the table instead of out of your hand. Some dogs have a little trouble here. The normal human reaction is to pinch harder. The solution is keeping the pinch the same light intensity for a longer period of time, until Pup grabs the dowel off the table.

7. Continue for several sessions until Pup is automatically fetching the dowel from the table upon command without the toe pinch.

8. Give Pup a session on the table with a light ear pinch instead of the toe pinch. The proper way to use ear pinch is to grasp Pup's collar with your hand. Then fold his ear back against the collar. Lightly press your thumbnail against the ear, pinning it against the collar. Press just hard enough that Pup becomes uncomfortable and fidgets a little. Then put the dowel in front of his mouth and wait for him to grab it. Release the pinch when he does.

9. Give Pup a session or two on the ground with a light ear pinch using first the dowel and then a dummy.

FORCE-FETCH TRAINING WITHOUT THE TABLE

If you choose to force-fetch train without the table, you should go through the same sequence of steps as with the table method. The major difference is that the dog is started on the ground, with the ear pinch instead of the toe pinch.

THE MOST COMMON MISTAKES

The most common mistakes that beginning trainers make are:

1. Using too much force. The trainer applies the pinch and doesn't get an immediate response, so he pinches harder. Some dogs will respond by shutting down and doing nothing. The correct method is to apply the light pinch. It should be just hard enough that Pup is uncomfortable. Then provide the escape route for him, by making sure that he gets the dowel in his mouth, which makes the pinch cease. Speed is not a requirement. Keep the pinch at the same intensity and wait for the response to occur. Use more time, not more force.

2. Skipping steps in the sequence will make it difficult for some dogs to get the picture. When Pup is not progressing, simplify. If he's not grabbing for the dowel, slip it into his mouth and release the pinch so he learns what turns off the pinch. Whenever you encounter problems, simplify.

3. Don't think that the command produces the response. You produce the response with the pinch. Only after the response is reliably occurring do you start preceding it with the "fetch" command. That's how Pup learns.

4. Many beginning trainers get wrapped up in the pinching and forget the power of reward. Just because the pinch is working, don't neglect the reward following the correct response. Petting and praise following the correct response increase the effectiveness of the force-fetch training process tenfold.

CHAPTER 19

TRAINING TWO
OR MORE DOGS

TODAY YOU NEVER see dogs worked in a group of two or more. The early trainers quite commonly worked dogs in a group. They left them sitting together in a group while the birds were shot or the dummies thrown, and called each dog over

Working dogs in groups has several advantages. It saves time and energy, for you and the dogs. Also, it's a good way to impress your friends.

individually when it was that dog's turn to work. The other dogs in the group were expected to sit calmly and honor the working dog. This practice made for superbly steady and obedient dogs. You still see this practice in England, but it has practically disappeared in America.

Training two or three dogs is much easier than training one. There are several advantages:

1. Each dog becomes more steady and obedient because he regularly exercises his self-control while watching the other dogs retrieve. He gets a lot more practice at honoring.

2. Each dog is less likely to be overworked, since the trainer has two or three dogs to spend time on. Usually the trainer feels like he needs to work for half an hour or an hour. That is generally too much training for a single dog.

3. It is quicker. It takes less time because the trainer doesn't have to walk out to pick up all those non-retrieves.

4. It is easier on the dogs and the trainer because the trainer doesn't have all his expectations riding on one dog. When he's training two or three, he can be more objective and thus a more effective trainer.

5. It will impress the heck out of your hunting companions. They see you sit two or three dogs, walk out and throw some dummies, and then call one dog out to work while the others sit quietly. They will see you take two dogs hunting and selectively send one to make each retrieve. They will think you're the best dog trainer around.

Here is how you train dogs in pairs:
1. Train each dog separately through the first ten or so obedience lessons.

2. Then start training them as a pair. The key point is to sit them far enough apart that you can project a signal to one dog without the other dog reading it as his.

3. Imagine yourself as standing at the center of a clock face. Place dog A fifteen feet away from you at twelve o'clock. Place the dog B away from you at three o'clock.

4. Throw a few dummies and pick them up yourself, leaving the dogs sitting in their respective places. After you have picked up the dummies, walk back to each dog successively and give each a few strokes on the shoulder, along with the praise "good dog." You

Sit the dogs far enough apart so that you can give a signal to one without the other reading it as his.

want to reward them for having sat quietly while you were throwing dummies and picking them up.

5. Return to your place at the center of the clock face. With your left hand, give a pronounced traffic cop "stop" gesture to dog A at twelve o'clock. While keeping your eyes on dog A, gently call dog B to you from his three o'clock position.

While giving dog A the traffic cop gesture, call dog B to you by using only his name.

Call B to you by using only his name. As you say his name, dip your right shoulder toward him to provide a visual signal. After a few repetitions, his name will become his signal to come. When dog B gets to you, stroke him gently on his shoulders and then take him back to his starting point. Walk over to dog A and stroke him gently on the shoulders.

6. Go through the same sequence several times, alternately calling A or B to you by name while keeping the other dog sitting with the traffic cop gesture and a threatening stare. After several sessions they will be used to coming when called and you can move them closer together.

7. After the two dogs are proficient at coming when called, and are foolproof on staying when the other's name is called, you can move on to the next phase of teaching them to honor each other's retrieves. For the first few retrieves, sit the dogs fifteen or twenty feet apart so that each can eas-

ily interpret your body language. As the dogs sit in place, throw a few dummies and pick them up yourself. Go over and stroke each dog on the shoulder with a "good dog." Then throw a dummy out and, after pausing a few seconds, call dog A to you by name. Sit him beside you, then unobtrusively send him for the dummy while you keep your eyes on dog B to help him stay in place. Give each dog a

Have the other dogs stay, while you send one dog to fetch the dummy.

couple of retrieves in this fashion, and finish up by throwing a couple of dummies that you pick up yourself. Over the next few sessions you can move the dogs closer together as they become more obedient and steady on honoring.

8. As the dogs become more adept at working as a pair you can add shooting, then birds. After a sufficient number of lessons, the dogs will be steady enough that you can take them duck hunting or dove hunting and work the pair, sending each dog on alternate retrieves. Your hunting partners will be impressed.

As the dogs become steadier at honoring, you can move them closer together—just like when hunting out of a duck blind.

CHAPTER 20

PHEASANTS, DOVES, AND QUAIL

PHEASANTS

Retrievers are born pheasant hunters. You don't have to train them to hunt; you only have to train them to be under control. If you can train your dog to come to you every time you call him, under any circumstances, then you have trained him to pheasant hunt. All you have to do is take him pheasant hunting and keep him within fifteen yards so that all the birds he flushes will flush within range of your shotgun. Here is the way you do it.

First, train Pup to the point that he is totally consistent on coming to you. Then simply take him pheasant hunting. Every time he gets over fifteen yards from you, call him in. After a while he will automatically stay within fifteen yards, and every bird he flushes will be in range. He wants to hunt and has been denied the area outside fifteen yards, so he will automatically start sweeping from side to side, quartering. The quartering provides the only outlet for that hunting urge if you have denied him the out-front terrain past fifteen yards.

It is fairly easy to accomplish this pheasant quartering training when you're doing the real thing, because bird scent is the necessary ingredient to bring out the hunter in Pup. Conversely, it is difficult to do this training in a contrived, artificial training setup. Without the bird scent and the excitement of hunting, Pup will tend to get bored quickly. If you want to produce the quartering behavior in an artificial environment, be sure to lay plenty of scent and make sure Pup periodically finds a bird. You can use pen-raised pheasants, dizzied pigeons, or clipped-wing ducks to lend realism to the quartering training exercise.

DOVES

Retrievers are great for dove hunting, but dove hunting is dangerous for retrievers. The popular southern sport of dove shooting is frequently fast and furious and thus can be dangerous for your dog. When the temperature is above 80 degrees Fahrenheit and the humidity is high, Pup is a candidate for a heat stroke, which is often fatal. To help protect Pup from heat stroke, follow these basic precautions.

Heat is the big enemy in dove hunting. Pup doesn't sweat through his skin and thus is deprived of the evaporative cooling that humans enjoy. He loses heat mainly through the evaporation of the surface area of his mouth and tongue. This limits his heat dissipation capacity, so you need to take an active role in keeping him from overheating in hot weather during strenuous activities such as training and dove hunting.

The most important thing you can do to help protect Pup from heat stroke is to moderate and regulate his physical activity. Running and retrieving generate a lot of heat in Pup's body. Moderating Pup's physical activity helps control his temperature. Don't give three or four strenuous retrieves in a row. Give him one retrieve, and then let him sit quietly for ten to fifteen minutes to get rid of some of the generated heat before sending him on the next retrieve.

One practice that will help Pup stay cool is for you to do some of the retrieving. When you knock down a bird that is easy to find, leave Pup sitting and go get it yourself. This practice will help Pup stay cool, and will also contribute mightily to his steadiness and calmness.

Another good way to dissipate heat is to put Pup in the water. If there is a pond near the dove field, try to station yourself near it. Put Pup in the water occasionally to cool him off. When Pup is in the pond, the water acts as a heat sink and sucks off body heat. When he emerges from the pond, the water on his coat evaporates and gives him the benefit of evaporative cooling over the total surface area of his body.

If there is not a pond handy, take a big jug of water on your dove shoot. Wet Pup down before you start, and periodically during the shoot. Pup will get more cooling effect from evaporation of water from his total skin surface area than he will get from drinking water.

The general rule for heat protection for retrievers on dove shooting is to keep them damp, and keep their activity levels low.

QUAIL

At the southeastern quail plantations you see more and more retrievers being used to pick up downed quail. At the more affluent establishments, Pup will be riding on the wagon. In other cases, Pup will be at heel by the guide. The word is spreading that retrievers are better at finding dead birds than are setters or pointers. Retrievers have been selectively bred to find dead birds, and they love to root around in a small area hunting up a dead bird.

Pointers and setters, on the other hand, have been selectively bred to find another covey of live birds. They do not like to stay in a small area hunting up dead birds. Upland dogs like to get on with the search for the next covey of live birds. You generally have to do a lot of arguing with a bird dog to keep him in a small area hunting up a dead bird.

You have already trained your retriever for quail hunting when you trained him to heel, because the appropriate place for Pup in quail hunting is at heel. Take a setter or pointer to find the coveys and do the pointing. After the birds are pointed, flushed, and shot, release Pup from heel to hunt up the dead birds.

If you want to hunt quail solely with a retriever, you can, but this is not one of Pup's stronger talents. To hunt quail you have to use Pup as a flusher, just as you do on pheasants. Keep him within fifteen yards and keep your eye on him. When he starts acting birdy, get ready for an impending flush.

Most retrievers will show a brief approximation of a pointing response, but it is minimal compared to an upland bird dog. Most retrievers, when they get within a critical distance of a live bird, will freeze for a split second before they pounce on the bird. This distance is around eighteen inches, so it requires a very tight-sitting bird for the freeze response to occur.

You could train this response into a full-fledged point if you spent enough time and had sufficient training skills, but it would be a lot easier to simply get a bird dog like a pointer or setter. An upland dog has most of the pointing behavior bred into him and requires much less training, and makes a much better quail dog. Retrievers should be reserved for the job of finding the shot birds.